A Chasm Crossing Church

By Michael Shaw

Published by Michael Shaw (Copyright 2015)

Printed by Create Space

ISBN-13: 978-0968100059

Library and Archives Canada Cataloguing in Publication

Shaw, Michael, 1963-, author
    A chasm crossing church / Michael Shaw.

Includes bibliographical references.
ISBN 978-0-9681000-5-9 (paperback)

    1. Church and the world. 2. Church renewal. 3. Christianity--21st century. I. Title.

| BR115.W6S43 2015 | 261'.1 | C2015-906161-X |

Table of Contents

Preface 5
Acknowledgements 7
Introduction 9
Part 1   How Bad Is the Chasm? 11
   Chapter 1 - Hearts Transformed 13
   Chapter 2 - Falling Numbers 27
   Chapter 3 - Church Health 39
   Chapter 4 - New Market 55
   Chapter 5 - Preparing Minds 69
Part 2   The Five Seismic Shifts 79
   Chapter 6 - Modern Science 81
   Chapter 7 - Productive Society 97
   Chapter 8 - Human Freedom 107
   Chapter 9 - Individual Truth 115
   Chapter 10 - Digitally Connected 123
Part 3   How to Cross the Chasm 131
   Chapter 11 - Crossing Over 133
   Chapter 12 - Digital Offering 145
   Chapter 13 - Electronic Bulletins 155
   Chapter 14 - Preaching Makeover 167
   Chapter 15 - Chasm Crossers 177
   Conclusion 187
   References 189

Preface

Living in a different time

Recently my father has been writing a book about his life that he has entitled *A Legend in my Own Mind*. As I read about his years growing up, I came face to face with a world I never knew. He entered full-time ministry in the early 1960s and there was still a lot of respect for the position of pastor in the community at large, even among people who were not church members. I have tried to imagine what it would have been like to live at that time; to attend a church when most of the neighborhood does the same thing every week. I cannot comprehend it. In one generation, the social landscape has changed so much that he might as well be describing a different country. As I have contemplated the huge changes that have taken place since then, it has filled me with a compassion for those in our churches who are trying to deal with the changes that have happened.

My purpose in writing this book is to help people who want their church to connect to the current culture and new generations, but do not know how to accomplish this. The gap between many of those in the church and those outside has grown spectacularly. It is my hope that this book will help you better understand why this gap is unique and assure you there is hope.

As part of the preparation process I visited a variety of churches in my local area. I soon realized that many congregations were in worse shape than I had suspected. I was well aware of declining numbers and the resulting financial squeeze, but I had not expected the lack of awareness regarding the tectonic shifts (large earth-shaking changes) that have occurred in society. My original intention had been to focus on how churches could create virtual communities, but realized that many people in churches needed to understand at a deeper level, what is really happening. This became my new goal.

My background as a technologist, teacher and theologue has been critical to my ability to identify the issues and provide a bird's-eye view of the cultural shifts that have had such a dramatic impact on the church world.

The first section, "How Bad Is the Chasm?" explains how very serious the situation is for the Church. The next one, "The Five Seismic Shifts," will show how a unique set of circumstances has led to where the Canadian Church is today. Finally, "How to Cross the Chasm" will give some guidelines and ideas on how to respond effectively.

The situation in which Christians in the West find ourselves, did not happen overnight. The Canadian church has been experiencing a deep cultural marginalization of the church for a long time (Nelson 2009, 96). It will take significant effort and prayer to become socially relevant again.

Acknowledgements

I would like to thank Stephen McMullin for his guidance and help as I created the foundations for this book as a project for my Master of Arts in Theology Degree.

Introduction

What the book is about

This book is intended to help people in the church understand the shifts that have happened in society. Understanding what has happened will assist churches as they attempt to reconnect to the culture around them. It will enable them to be missional to those outside the church in a way that makes sense to secular people in society. A huge part of being missional is figuring out what the language, values, customs, beliefs, history and ideals are in the culture you are trying to reach. Western society has changed so much that it is, in many ways, a foreign culture to those who live in the church world. When missionaries are sent overseas to minister to other people groups, they must study the culture they are going into, in order to be effective witnesses for Christ. North American Christians have a responsibility to evaluate Western culture in exactly the same way and seek to understand it.

There are many important elements in the creation of a healthy congregation that is able to cross the chasm between church and culture. Depending on the power of God and prayer is critical. Admitting our sin and lack of faith is critical. Modifying church structures to enable ministry, instead of fighting against it, is critical. Leaders who love the people and are willing to take strong stands when necessary, are critical.

Cultivating a missional vision for how the church can impact the community is critical. Depending on the authority of scripture is critical. Listening to the Holy Spirit is critical.

The fact that this book will not talk very much about these things does not make them any less important, but many resources on how to do these things have been created by others. This book focuses on the gap in understanding by church people about exactly what has happened. The purpose of the first third of the book is to help church people understand that a chasm between church and culture exists. The second third identifies ways that shifts in thinking have created the current culture. The final third provides examples that are intended to get you thinking about the kinds of changes that will be necessary in order to reconnect.

Part 1

How Bad Is the Chasm?

Part 1 of this book talks about how bad the chasm is between people in the church and people in the world. This gap is not just that, on any given Sunday, church people are in church and secular people are not. It is related, instead, to the vastly different ways that people in the two groups think. These differences create a gulf between the two groups. If churches in the West refuse to deal with this new reality, they will die. Fortunately, it does not have to be this way and Christian churches can adapt to this new challenge and flourish.

Chapter 1 - Hearts Transformed

Summary

The reason for the chasm between church people and secular people is ideological, and every effort to cross this chasm must be based on a solid theological foundation. We must experience forgiveness by God and the righteousness given to us by Christ. We must be led by the Holy Spirit and experience the love of God the Father. Our minds need to be transformed to believe that, with God, all things are possible. We need to change our focus from ourselves, to the mission that we are called to do. We must allow God to really change our hearts and be a people called by Him.

The Chasm is not Empty Pews

The church is facing a chasm. Many congregations that were once vibrant and alive now find themselves in trouble with falling church attendance. On average weekly church attendance in Canada is down over 50% since the end of World War II (Bibby 2012, 5). In many congregations, it seems like an entire generation is missing. The number of younger people indicating they are religiously unaffiliated has reached 29% (Pew 2013).

The chasm we face is not just an attendance issue. The truth is, it is possible to get more people in the pews and still not solve the problem. The real chasm is centered in ideas and how people think.

The chasm the church is facing as a result of the multiple shifts that have taken place in the ideological realm. People in normal society have begun to think differently. The lack of people in church on Sunday is, in many ways, a product of the seismic shifts in thinking that have occurred, not primarily a sign of a generation that lacks commitment or is not interested in spiritual things. In fact, there is evidence to suggest that young people today are more interested in spiritual things than the previous generation was (Bibby 2012, 6). The problem is we are not speaking the same language and therefore have done a very poor job of representing the exciting gospel to a new generation.

Much of this book will discuss what the seismic shifts in thinking have been and what can be done about them, but first it is important to address the spiritual side of renewal.

Renewal must always have a Spiritual Foundation

All of the knowledge that individuals or congregations gain from this book will be worthless if they do not appreciate that real spiritual transformation is essential for any substantive change to take place in churches. The lives of believers must be transformed as they allow the Holy Spirit to change them. They must seek God in prayer and allow the scriptures to inform their thinking. Jesus must truly be made Lord of their lives.

We must turn away from the worldliness that causes us to separate ourselves from God. It is essential to stop participating in activities that damage our witness and place stumbling stones in the paths of others who are actively searching for the truth. Church members must truly come to understand the full implications of the Gospel and how it is the Good News of God's forgiveness and grace.

Accepting the gift of forgiveness

In April of 1969, my father, who was the minister at Port Williams United Baptist Church in Nova Scotia, was asked to speak at a couple of special services that were to take place at a nearby church. He entitled his message "Captured by Christ" and it was based on 2 Corinthians 5:1-15. Although I was only five years old, he brought me with him.

During the second service, at Billtown United Baptist Church, a kind lady leaned over and asked if I wanted a peppermint. I said yes, but not just to the peppermint; I was saying yes to everything I was hearing. On the ride home with my father, I could feel a new love and joy welling up inside me. I was not sure what was going on, so I asked my parents and they told me I had accepted Jesus. My heart had been changed.

There are people in the church who have never accepted the completed work of Christ. They may be good attenders and givers. They may be on committees and boards. They may be even leaders of programs and events, but they have never really understood or accepted the gift of Jesus.

Addressing the chasm is not for the faint of heart and without the sustaining love of Jesus in our life we will soon shrink back in fear. It is critical that the congregation be presented with the compelling need to allow Jesus to become their Savior. This is not all about just presenting more and more teaching within the confines of a holy huddle; outreach is also important. Often it is only as we try to reach out to others that we come face to face with the lack of love contained within our own souls. Our limited spiritual resources become apparent and the opportunity for real heart change appears.

Righteous in Christ

I was discussing various topics with my co-workers during a break when the topic of the church came up. One of them looked me right in the eye and said, "Do you think people in group G are going to Hell?" I paused for a moment and replied, "Although it is not understood by people outside the church or by very many inside the church, authentic Christianity would say that all of us and every single group will go to Hell." I could see that my words were a bit of a shock. They had fully expected reasons for why one group was more sinful than another and were prepared with counter arguments, but this caught them off guard. "So you are saying we are going to Hell?" queried another co-worker tentatively. "All of our works deserve death, including mine," I responded. "The only one who does not deserve death is Jesus. If we trust in what He has done, we can be saved."

In many churches, there are people who think that the purpose of the church is to help them become righteous, that we need to do good things to others, because that is what God requires. Although it is very true that God does want us to love others, scripture is very clear that by ourselves we do not have the capacity to love them.

Romans 3:23 says, "For all have sinned and fall short of the glory of God." This does not mean that we were sinners until we accepted Jesus and now we sin no more. This means, we fell short, by our own efforts, to meet the righteous requirements of God before we accepted Christ, and we continue to do so. Our righteousness must always be based on what He has done, not on our own attempts at holiness. We are justified not because of what we do, but because of the gift of God. We have been redeemed by God, through Christ Jesus, and this is what makes us acceptable.

Some may argue that the Apostle James says, "Faith without deeds is dead." Notice however, what James is trying to do by his works. He says in James 2:18, "... I will show you my faith by my deeds." In other words, he is not trying to demonstrate by his deeds that he is acceptable to God, but that the deeds demonstrate the faith he already has inside of him regarding what Jesus has done.

Christ brings life

The pastor's sermon was just getting started, but already the message was clear: You need to work. A series of things that needed to be done was soon listed and our flimsy excuses for opting out were mocked. Where is the life I wondered? Is guilt our only weapon to motivate the troops and get them going? It is my conjecture that the only effective and long-term solution is to allow ourselves to be transformed by the life of Christ.

There are those in the church that have indeed accepted Christ as their Savior. They see that Jesus covers their sin and it is by the grace of God that they have been adopted into God's family. Yet it is at this very important juncture that many make a fatal mistake. They now try, by their own human effort and willpower, to live their lives for Christ. The problem is, we can never live a life that is worthy.

Christ came, not only to cover us with His blood so our sins would be forgiven, but also to give us life. It is not our life that we must live, but we must allow Jesus to live His life through us. The apostle Paul summarized this very well when he said in Galatians 2:20, "I have been crucified with Christ and I no longer live, but Christ lives in me."

Churches must not only become places of forgiveness, but also places of life, where congregants allow the life of the living Jesus to flow out of them to others. Some might say we can't wait for this, because important work needs to get done; but could it be that, perhaps, there are things we are doing in our churches that are not what God wants, and maybe some of these activities need to stop? Perhaps it is more important, from God's perspective, that we love each other with His gift of love.

Hearts Transformed

Spirit Led

I was really looking forward to the party being held by Acadia Christian Fellowship and hoping my car did not act up so I could get to it. My car engine carburetor kept sticking in the cold weather, causing the accelerator to get stuck full on. Just at the point I saw the students come out of the residence and get in the car I was supposed to follow, my car engine started screaming again. I rushed to fix the engine by popping the hood and resetting the carburetor, but I was losing them. I managed to follow them up a hill, but then they were gone.

As I went up and down the streets looking for the vehicle that would let me know where the party was, I became more and more upset. My carburetor had gotten stuck again and I knew that, in my own strength, I would never find the party. In my frustration, I called out to God for help and suddenly I heard something in my head say, *go right*, so I turned right. I heard *right* again, then *right* again, then *left*, then *right*, then *left*, then *right* and each time I took the appropriate road. As I turned the last corner, I looked up and there in front of me was the car I had been supposed to follow.

This is a rather dramatic example of following the Spirit of God and it doesn't happen to me very often. What does happen to me more regularly is the still small voice of the Holy Spirit speaking to my spirit. As Christ followers, we must be open to the leading of God's Spirit, in both the dramatic and quiet ways. We must follow the Spirit, as the normal everyday way of doing church, and stop depending on ourselves. Just as I had no hope but to call on God to find my way, so, crossing the chasm between the church and society will require us to be led by the Spirit of God.

Love of the Father

I was driving back to work one day and I started listening to a woman talking on Christian radio. I had tuned in part way through, so I missed some of the details, but I did come to understand that her son was in prison for murdering someone and she had come to speak at the facility where he was incarcerated. She explained that she told her story for a while and then invited her husband to come and share just a bit about his experience. It was while this loving father talked about the love and pain he had gone through with his son that the hearts of the prisoners broke. As they started to cry, the father went on to explain that, although they probably do not have a father like him, they do have a Heavenly Father who loves them.

There are many people in churches who are still working to try to win a father's approval. This transfers over to them trying to win God's approval and they try, in their own strength, to work toward what they think God wants them to do. They take the free gift of God's love and forgiveness and convert it to a 'works' mentality. In their eyes, they become justified in the sight of God, not because of what Christ has done for them, but because of what they do for Christ.

In order to change our thinking in this area, it is critical that people come to understand and experience the loving heart of God the Father. We need to live knowing we are totally loved by a Heavenly Father who desires only good things for us. It is His love that pours into us and then pours out to others. Our churches must become the kinds of communities in which the love of our compassionate Heavenly Father is felt by all who participate.

Transformed minds

I was talking with a real prayer warrior in the church who loves to have people come to her home so she can pray for them. As the conversation turned to the new generation and their lack of interest in attending church she said, "They will never come, they are just not interested. We might as well just make a service that the older people will enjoy."

Like her, many people in churches have given up hope that things can change. They look at the circumstances they find themselves in and, quite rightly, conclude that in the natural realm, there does not seem to be any way to fix the decline of their church. This discouragement leads to a lack of faith and we doubt that even God can do anything about it.

Our minds need to be transformed by the power of God. We need, as churches, to stop looking at the poor natural circumstances and start looking at the riches of God that are ours in Christ. The apostle Paul tells us in Ephesians 3:16, "I pray that out of His glorious riches he may strengthen you with power through his Spirit in your inner being."

Trying to save our churches in our own strength is an impossible task. Allowing God to change our hearts and make us into his Holy people is the only solution. When people see how we have been changed, then they too will want to come and worship the God that makes a difference.

Missionally Focused

I was a part of a small group at our church that was tasked with identifying ways that the congregation could reach out to the surrounding community. As we began to talk about how we could do missions, one participant remarked that she just could not get world missions out of her mind. "I know that when we say 'missions' we are talking about the local community," she said, "but in my mind, all I can think about is missions overseas."

For many in the church, missions has meant some exotic location overseas. We send missionaries there and they are helping people who are worse off than we are. There is an implicit, underlying assumption that our nation does not need the kind of help we are giving others; a belief that our nation is essentially Christian and, although it is our duty to give to local charities, we do not have to reach our community with the message of Christ. The people around us have plenty of churches from which to choose; they just need to pick one and start attending.

Although many church members might not admit it, they have a "come to us" mentality. This approach was somewhat effective in North America in the 1950's when most people attended church on Sunday, but in today's culture, it is severely deficient. Our churches must develop a mentality that sees mission as something local and that sees the local community as a mission field to which we are called to go.

It is important not to try and bring about this change via the mechanism of guilt. Instead, it requires a two-pronged approach of vision and heart transformation. The people need to have a vision for what God is calling them to do locally and members' hearts need to be filled with compassion for those who do not know God.

Changing for others

There may be some who do not believe we should change how we present the message of the Bible and that any change we make actually compromises the Word of God. The reality is that, from the very beginning, the timeless truths of God were presented in a way that was adapted to the listening audience. The truth is still the truth, but listeners cannot understand it if it is not presented in a way they can comprehend it.

The Apostle Paul took it to the extent that he actually made himself like the people he was trying to reach. He says in 1 Corinthians 9:19, "Though I am free and belong to no one, I have made myself a slave to everyone, to win as many as possible." He became like the people He was trying to reach, not forcing them to cross over the cultural chasm to him; but instead, changing himself, that they might more easily receive the message. In our congregations, we need to speak the language of the culture around us and this means we need to change.

When Paul came to a new place, he always spoke to the people using language and references they could understand; he adapted the message of Jesus to new surroundings. For example, when addressing the people of Athens, he said, "'For in him we live and move and have our being.' As some of your own poets have said, 'We are his offspring'" (Acts 17:28). He brought pagan philosophers into the conversation in order to clarify the message for his listeners.

Churches must be willing to change in order for the message of Jesus to be properly heard. Holding on to a particular version, of the Bible because we believe it to be more spiritual, is neither helpful nor biblical. We must be willing to change, so others may come to know the truth about God and the wonderful gift He has given us in His Son.

Heart Change

My wife told me that she had forwarded me an email. I opened it and it was from a lady I knew who had been going through a real struggle in her life. She indicated that the message I had preached in church that morning, about how it was actually better for us that Jesus went away, instead of staying on earth with us, was really working on her heart. I was glad to hear that God was bringing about some real healing in her life.

If we want churches to be chasm-crossing, we must have a heart change. We must allow our hearts to be changed by God, in order for us to have anything that we can offer to others. If we have not experienced the transforming power of God, how can we promote it as the solution? A heart change in our churches is critical.

The gap that must be crossed is both huge and unique, and in our own strength we will certainly fail, but if we trust God to change us and fill us with the Spirit of God, we will able to cross over. It will still require effort on our part, but with God, all things are possible.

God among us

At its core, the church must be a gathered people who come together physically, and today, even electronically, who have been and are being transformed by the power of God. If real heart change is not occurring among the people, then they are not ready for the journey.

The goal cannot be to transform the world into a replica of the existing church with all its traditions, but to see people, both in the church and in the world, being impacted by the love of God. It is the mercy and grace of God that must become manifest in our midst.

There is no way to see renewal in the church without a spiritual foundation. At the same time, the challenges that churches face today are different than they have been in the past. We still need to engage in spiritual disciplines, confessing sins and prayer, but this chasm is new and it will require more from us than this.

Chapter 2 - Falling Numbers

Summary

Urgency is critical if we want to deal appropriately with the cultural shifts that have occurred in society. To generate this urgency we must come face to face with the real numbers of church decline. We must not fool ourselves into thinking this can be solved by minor changes. Going back to what we have done in the past will not fix it. Prayer without action will not make a difference. Adding more programs will not help. Overcoming the fear of witnessing will not bring about the change we are looking for. The chasm is huge and we must evaluate it to come to grips with the problem we face. We must accept that we have a big problem that is not going away, not blame each other for the mess we are in, but put our energy into finding a way out and a way up.

Countdown to Closure

I had heard about this congregation before I went to see them and what I heard was, in a word, "trouble". Numbers were down, average age of members was climbing, finances were falling and any real connection to the community was being lost. As I sat down to observe the service, I am not sure what I expected, but I guess I thought there would be some concern and perhaps a pinch of fear. Instead, an air of contentment and satisfaction pervaded the place. Suddenly, I realized that they were happy with their little fellowship, just the way it was.

One thing that constantly surprises me is the lack of urgency I find in many churches. From churches that are in trouble, but not in critical condition, I find people who are relatively happy with their church. Those churches that are in real trouble seem to exude a sadness for the past, but little angst that things need to change now. I do not know if this behavior is primarily a result of a defense mechanism against the truth of the situation, the mistaken belief that God really does have only one specific way He wants church done, or an ignorance of the huge cultural shifts that have occurred. Perhaps, it is a combination of all three.

To help churches get over these barriers, we need to generate urgency by lovingly helping the congregation see exactly how bad things really are. Change is not easy, but without a sense of urgency, it is almost impossible. In this chapter, I will provide some evidence for how bad the situation is generally, and in the next chapter, I cover the tools to evaluate your specific congregation.

Falling Numbers

Here are some yearly totals of members received by baptism for all churches that are a part of the Atlantic Baptist Convention. This is the denomination of the church I attend. I have averaged the years 2009-2013 and the period ten years earlier 1999-2003.

2013 - 482	2003 - 810
2012 - 381	2002 - 924
2011 - 426	2001 - 831
2010 - 513	2000 - 849
2009 - 527	1999 - 942
--------------	--------------
Avg. = 465.8	Avg. = 871.2
(Reid 2014, SM-18)	(Gardner 2002, SM-22)

What this shows is a 46% drop in the number of baptisms in just 10 years. This is a very serious decline and one that is shared by many other church groups.

The Western church is in a difficult situation and on some level this has been recognized in churches. In response to this a number of different approaches have been tried to address this issue. Here are four fairly typical responses that churches make.

We will go back to the past and that will fix it

I knew something was wrong when I went to the website of the church I was going to visit that week and the pastor was no longer listed. It indicated that they had a special speaker, but no other clues as to what was going on. On Sunday, my son and I were a bit late, but we did manage to slip into a pew just before the service started. I took my usual notes as things went on and then partway through the service, the church clerk stood up to give a report that indicated that the church had recently gone through a process of discovery and had finally found what it really wanted to be about. No further information was given so it was not clear to me what had happened.

A more detailed picture was revealed the next week when I talked to a member of the church. They told me that the minister (no longer with the church) and the deacon's (who were soon to leave as well) had been trying to reach out to the community, but many of the older members did not like this. They wanted things to be the way they used to be; to go back to the older music and stop playing the modern stuff.

I personally love singing hymns and believe many of them contain powerful theological messages. A traditional service is no problem for me, because I grew up in the church; but for most people today, this will not work. Trying to recreate the past in an effort to make a better future is not possible. It is true that, for a short time, a church may be able to bring in mature members from other churches who like the old formats, but sooner or later this plan will fail.

We will not be able to connect to the world today by creating a church that is a perfect representation of the past. The gulf between what current members find meaningful and what secular people need is vast. Old hymns just do not communicate clearly or meaningfully to most people today.

We will pray and God will fix it

As I sat in the pew of yet another church, I heard once again the refrain: "God will bring people back to church." There was a murmuring of agreement and the slight nods of a number of graying heads. "We must be faithful to the Truth," continued the speaker, "and God will bring in the harvest." Looking around at the gaping holes of empty pews in the church I thought to myself, if this is true, then either they are not faithful or God is doing a poor job.

I started listening again, "We need to pray and ask God to move in our church. God is powerful and if we depend on Him, we will see great things happen. We must get on our knees and pray for the power of God to come." A clear, "Amen," came from the back corner. I sighed quietly and braced myself to hear more about how only God can take us out of the trouble we are in.

Now, I do believe that it is only through the power of God that we can be changed spiritually and have our hearts transformed. We serve a miracle-making God and He will show us the way. When we call out to Him, He will hear us. There are times the answer may not be what we want, but other times we will be astounded at what happens. However, as important as it is to pray, it is critically important that we also do something physically. In the current social situation we find ourselves in, it is not enough to think prayer alone is the entire answer to our problem. There are things that we must learn and do, to have a hope of reaching normal people in the world.

We will add better programs and that will fix it

As I entered the church the minister was explaining how critical it is to have vision in a church. Having a vision, he explained, allows you to prioritize what you want to do. It was all good stuff, but as the session continued, I wondered to myself if the church would be courageous enough to cut particular church activities, if they did not match up with the vision. I remembered hearing some of the executives at Apple say that one of the hardest things they have to do is deciding what not to do, how they found it difficult to only commit to projects that can be done well.

As the meeting continued it seemed like the real goal was not to clarify vision, but to identify new programs the church could get involved in. I got the feeling that people felt that if only we were to add some really good and new programs, things would turn around for this church.

Adding more and more without cutting anything out, is a sure way to guarantee burnout in the pastoral staff and for the church members. We really need to identify what programs in our churches God wants to continue and which ones he wants to die.

Having good programs is critical. I attended a church once that prided itself in only doing what God wanted. The preaching was powerful and there was a real concern to discern God's will. The problem was, the programs were bad. People allowed things to slip because they were afraid of going against what God wanted. The sentiment was that if God wants people to lead Sunday school, He will tell them. The problem is this just does not work well in practice.

Congregations and their leaders need to identify the programs God wants them to concentrate on and then put effort into these areas to do an excellent job. Too often, churches try to keep programs going that should have stopped and they wind up doing a mediocre job on everything, instead of an excellent job on a few things.

In the end, however, even if we do manage to get some excellent programs going, this will still not be enough. The chasm that has opened up between church people and normal people is just too great. It cannot be crossed by programs alone, without us understanding the new social reality. We must have a better understanding of how thinking in society has changed.

We will start witnessing and that will fix it

It was a big event and a special speaker had been brought to the church to provide an uplifting message. Just wait till you hear her, people told me, she is really good. As she started her sermon, I could see that she was very well spoken. "You better watch out," she said, "we have been praying for you; praying that the fear of witnessing will be removed from the churches." Immediately I started wondering if fear was holding me back from witnessing. As I thought about it, I realized, at least for me, it was not fear of rejection that was the problem, but concern over the kind of church to which I would be inviting people. It is not so much that churches are full of hypocrisy, although that is a concern, but more because they are so very far out of touch with society and the issues that normal people face.

Turning my attention back to the sermon, I heard her say, "Once the fear of witnessing has been removed, we will see growth in our churches; when people are invited, they come." Will they, I wondered? I agreed that some people would come a time or two, but what would keep them coming back? I have to admit that there are times I have found church to be boring and tedious. I suspect that most normal people will quickly tire of what most churches have to offer.

I certainly agree that it is critical for people to be witnesses of the transforming power of Christ in their lives; witnessing about what God has done for us, not trying to convince others of the reality of God using logical arguments and apologetics.

Recently my denomination had some seminars on "Creating a Culture of Invitation." The idea is to have a Back to Church Sunday which will provide opportunities and perhaps a little push for people to invite friends and neighbours to church. Inviting others to church is an excellent way to begin to see some growth, but again, without some deeper changes in the church, it will only bring a temporary, short-term gain.

Even if we are able to train people to be fearless witnesses, so they can explain to others what God had done in their lives; even if we create structures like "Back to Church Sunday," it will not be enough. Dying churches must come to terms with the huge changes in society and how the church has to make huge changes in response.

Responding to the Challenge

We have now covered four common ways in which churches respond to the challenges presented by the changes in our society. Although there are elements in all of them that are very important, they each fall short of providing a framework that will help us effectively address the issues of today. We can all agree that witnessing is important and needs to happen. Creating excellent programs is also a very good thing.

Nothing we do will be totally effective until the true scope of the problem comes into view. It is only as we see the entirety of the task before us that we can respond appropriately and effectively.

So where do we start? Where does your church start? The answer to this is to begin by admitting that the strategies we have implemented to try and cope with the chasm are not working. We must admit to ourselves and others: "Houston, we have a problem." Accepting that you have a problem and that you cannot handle it, is the first step on the road to recovery.

As humans, we never like to confess that we have made a mistake, and at the best of times, it can be a real struggle for us to come to terms with what we have done wrong. It is even more difficult for a group to deal with its problems, and the church, in particular, has a real struggle with this. Some of us have gotten the idea into our heads that it would not be loving to talk about problems: just smile and wave and pretend everything will be all right, but we must not allow ourselves the comfort of falling into deception. It does not matter what the state of the building or finances are, if new people are not coming to faith.

In order for our churches to start on the proper path to recovery, we must really allow this message to sink in. There is a reason each AA meeting starts with the admission by each of the participants that they are Alcoholics. Our human tendency is to want to gloss over the painful problem and move on to other things. In particular, we like to start talking about potential solutions before we have really understood the problem.

It is critical to get everyone in a church community to agree that there is a problem. There is not any point in showing people exactly how bad the situation is (which is covered in more detail in upcoming chapters), if they are not willing to entertain the idea that perhaps they have been doing it wrong. If a church is in the denial mindset, then the leaders and those who see the reality of the situation must focus on helping the church face the truth.

Leaders must be careful at this point, so as not to unconsciously blame the church members for the situation. It is easy for leaders to slip into the mindset that the real reason for the failure of the church is a lack of authentic spirituality and commitment on the part of the members, thinking, if they worked as hard as I do then we would not have this problem. Sermons berating church members for not being "witnessing Christians" will never accomplish real change.

Congregants, in turn, must be careful not to blame the church leaders for failing to turn things around. It's easy to believe the real reason for the failure of the church is a lack of commitment and effectiveness on the part of the leaders, believing that if they did what we are paying them to do, we would not have this problem. Gossiping and ridiculing leaders for being ineffective and weak will never accomplish real change.

I am not saying that lack of member commitment and leadership ineffectiveness cannot be part of the problem, but that, given the huge chasm of societal challenges we are facing, they will almost always play a secondary role. Certainly these things need to be dealt with, but they are not solutions to our primary problem. It is a problem that can only be addressed by first admitting that it exists.

A good way to start is by presenting the positive vision of what the church should be: utilizing examples from the Bible that show what the early Christian church was like and, at the same time, starting to introduce some numbers that show graphically the decline of the congregation. Remember, at this point, we are not trying to get people to agree on the specifics of the problem or even to think of possible solutions. The goal is to get everyone to agree that there is a problem.

Pull up or we will crash

As I prepared to start the meeting of Instructional Assistants, I was determined that they would realize we were about to crash. This group had been picked without any input from me and I was stuck with the resulting mess. Not only were they not proficient with all the technology we were going to teach, but there were some huge personality conflicts among the five of them. I had already intervened in a number of situations that threatened to escalate to physical fights among them.

What made this situation the absolute worst was they refused to believe we had a problem. No matter how many times I explained to them what we had to do or how difficult the task was before us, they just shrugged it off. They had zero ownership of the problem and until they did, I knew we were going to go down in flames.

"Stand up and make your hands goggles and your arms wings like this," I said. "You are a plane and we are going to take off." I got them to do all the plane sounds and motions as I showed them an animation of a plane just barely managing to skim over the tops of mountains. These mountains represented the events that we had to successfully put on over the summer. Together we climbed, dove and looked foolish together. When we had made a successful flight, I said, "Unless we start working as a team, we are going to crash right into the side of one of those mountains and it will not be pretty."

For the very first time, I could see a glimmer of recognition of what we were facing; the beginnings of accepting the situation for what it was and finally realizing we had a problem, a really big problem. They came to know, finally, that we were a team and we would tackle it together.

Chapter 3 - Church Health

Summary

Many churches are in serious decline in membership and attendance (Roozen 2013, 10). I felt it was important to create a scale that could be used to identify the health of particular congregations. This scale, taken from a Casualty Triage Scale, helps to assess the health of churches on a scale from very poor to healthy. The colour black signifies congregations that are close to death, while the colour blue signifies congregations that are in the process of dying. Red indicates congregations that are doing poorly and yellow refers to congregations that need help. Green ones are the healthy churches. The vital signs used to find a church's position on the scale are the demographics of the congregation, attendance of members and the conversion rate of new believers. These factors can be used to provide a rough estimate of where any church falls on the scale. The hope is that, once church members see the reality of the situation, it may help them see the seriousness of the situation and enable them to overcome the resistance to change.

Where did the people go?

As I sat down in the big chair behind the pulpit, the congregation disappeared. The huge balcony had not been used for years, so there was no one up there. There was no one in the right hand section, no one in the left hand section and no one at the front of the center section. The few parishioners in attendance were clustered at the back of the center section, which was completely blocked from my view by the large wooden pulpit in front of me. I felt like I was completely alone in the church.

As I go from church to church in my local area, I find the majority of them are in bad shape with very few attending. There are a few churches that have sanctuaries over 50% full, but they are the exception to the general rule. What I am experiencing seems to be consistent with the data that is available for what is happening across Canada and the United States (Pew 2013).

Choosing a scale to evaluate the situation

In light of the precipitous decline in many churches, it will be helpful to provide a scale to help identify the relative health of particular congregations. It helps to know how healthy a church is, before trying to make changes. Three factors have been chosen to determine where a church falls on the scale: demographics, attendance and conversions. There are other factors that could be used, but these will provide clarity. These factors or vital signs will help to determine the relative condition of different churches.

This church health scale is simply a modified version of the Mass Casualty Triage Scale used by medical personnel to evaluate people who have been involved in a serious accident situation.

Mass Casualty Triage Scale

Priority Victims:
They will receive treatment and transportation in order of priority.

Priority 1 (Red)
Serious but salvageable life-threatening injury/illness

Priority 2 (Yellow)
Moderate to serious injury/illness (not immediately life-threatening)

Priority 3 (Green)
"Walking-wounded"

Non-Priority Victims:
They will not receive treatment or transportation.

Priority 4 (Blue)
Critical and potentially fatal injuries or illness.

Priority 5 (Black)
Clearly deceased at the scene with no vital signs or fatal injuries.

One might wonder, why choose this scale? The reason is that the situation is so critical among churches that this type of emergency scale is called for. If the situation does not change, many churches will die. It is important to determine which ones have a better chance of surviving and which ones do not so resources can be provided for these priority churches.

At the same time, even a dead church can be resurrected by God and we must always be prepared for God to do the miraculous. It may be that God directs us to pray for the revival of a church that, by all outward signs, is beyond hope. Perhaps, like the story of Lazarus in the Bible, God wants to clearly demonstrate His power.

Church Health Scale

(Vital signs are: Demographics, Attendance and Conversions)

Priority 1 (Red)
Church is in serious but salvageable condition with poor vital signs

Priority 2 (Yellow)
Church is in moderate condition with OK vital signs.

Priority 3 (Green)
Church is in relatively normal condition with good vital signs.

Priority 4 (Blue)
Church is in critical condition with very weak vital signs.

Priority 5 (Black)
Church is dying with all vital signs being very bad.

Now let us cover the Church Health Scale in more detail.

Black

A Priority 5 (Black) Church is basically dead with all vital signs (Demographics, Attendance and Conversions) being very bad.

Hopefully your church does not fall into this category, but many will. At this point, most of the church members and leadership have come to the realization that it is over. Typically, all financial resources have been exhausted trying to keep programs and the building going, but not always. There will be some churches that will have sufficient endowment funds to outlast all the members and potentially keep the building maintained. This is why finances have not been included as one of the vital signs. It is possible for a church to be dead and still have a substantial amount of money.

For this church, unless there is a miracle, it is over and it is time to wrap things up. If there are any resources remaining, they should be bequeathed to healthy churches. It may be very appropriate to plan a final service to honour the past and decommission the building. Certainly the church members will have to grieve the closure of the church and as much comfort should be provided to them as is possible.

Recognizing that a church is dead and taking the appropriate steps towards closure is a necessary duty. At the same time, we should never stop praying for a miracle: calling out to God in pain and sorrow, believing that even for dead churches, a resurrection is possible, because we follow a God of miracles.

Blue

A Priority 4 (Blue) Church is in critical condition with very weak vital signs.

This is the most difficult category to deal with. Many churches in this condition do not want to admit it and church members cling to the hope that their congregation is going to be okay. It may take someone coming in to the church to evaluate it and make the final verdict that, although there are some vital signs, it is in the process of dying.

The first task with this group is helping them come to the realization that the writing is on the wall. Many congregations will fight this and if that is the case, there is little that can be done. If, however, people are able to accept the verdict that the downward path the congregation is on will ultimately lead to its death, this will introduce the possibility of hope. Apart from God, it would seem best to just let this one go, but it may well be that God puts his finger on the congregation and says, "I am going to save this one."

Red

A Priority 1 (Red) Church is in serious, but salvageable condition, with poor vital signs.

This church has the potential to change and become healthy again, but time is running out. It will take significant outside help to bring this church around; if intervention does not happen quickly they will not live. This can be a tough sell to church members because they can still see good things happening in the congregation. "Look," they may say, "we are so much better off than the church down the street." This may be true, but comparing a somewhat unhealthy congregation with one that is dying does not mean it is healthy.

Members in such a church often think the most pressing issue that they need to deal with is finances. The truth is, spiritual issues, not financial ones, must become top priority. Until the core of what the church is about is stabilized, nothing else matters. It is very possible to win the battle for money, while at the same time losing the battle for faith.

Priority one for this church must now be to have the members grow spiritually. There may even be some long-time attenders who do not have a real relationship with Jesus. Helping people understand what the gospel is and applying it to their lives is key.

Yellow

A Priority 2 (Yellow) Church is in moderate condition with OK vital signs.

This church may appear to be doing very well, but there are hidden injuries that need to be addressed. It may be able to survive for some time on its own without outside intervention, but there is the danger that things could suddenly become more serious.

It is hard to convince a church in condition yellow that they need to change, just like it is for the red ones. The difference is that leaders of a church in the red category are facing so many issues day to day, they cannot deny that something is seriously wrong. Leaders of a church in the yellow category are able fool themselves into thinking everything is okay. The advantage these churches have is that once leaders agree something is wrong, it is easier for the congregation to deal with the problems. These churches will still need some outside support, but nothing like churches who are in the red category.

Often, in a church in the yellow category, doctrine and discipleship are in relatively good shape. The area it needs to focus on more is often missions. A lot of material has come out in the last few decades that has focused on the importance of missions. These resources have been very helpful and have enabled some churches to gain the proper perspective on why they exist. From the very beginning, churches have had a missional mandate and are tasked with helping others become disciples of Jesus Christ.

Green

A Priority 3 (Green) Church is in a relatively normal condition with good vital signs.

You are lucky if your church is in this category, because you are part of a very rare species. (Most churches who might place themselves in green are actually yellow or even red.) This church is in good condition. It is growing spiritually and numerically. It has solid discipleship and is reaching out in mission to the community around it. There is strong health here and this group only needs minor patching up.

The church in the green category has a demographic profile that is close to the population around it or skewed toward youth. It has solid attendance numbers, given the size of the current sanctuary, at over 80% full. There is also a solid conversion rate and a vibrant spiritual atmosphere where people are excited to worship Jesus.

This is a church that can immediately jump in and start dealing with chasm issues. It may already have been doing some of this, but hopefully this book will provide additional detail about things they should think about and do.

Vital Sign: Demographics

Of all the vital signs, Demographics is the most important and can be thought of as the heart rate of the church. Just as a doctor can look at the readout of an electrocardiogram and determine much about the health of a patient, so, analyzing a church's demographic profile speaks volumes regarding its overall state. Without even looking at the other two vital signs, you can almost guess where the church is going to wind up on the priority scale.

Black

Almost all the members are over 65 years old.

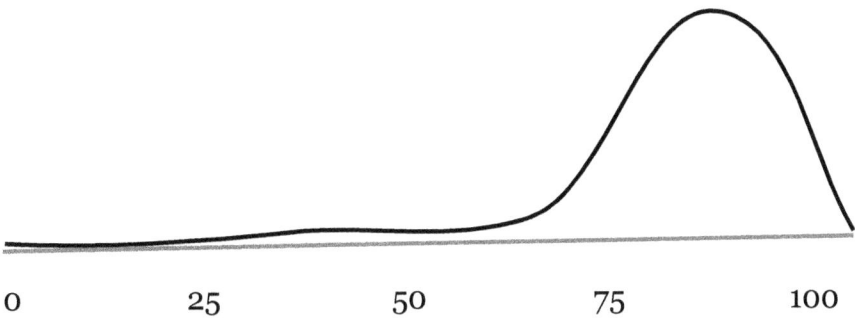

Blue

The vast majority of members are older than 50.

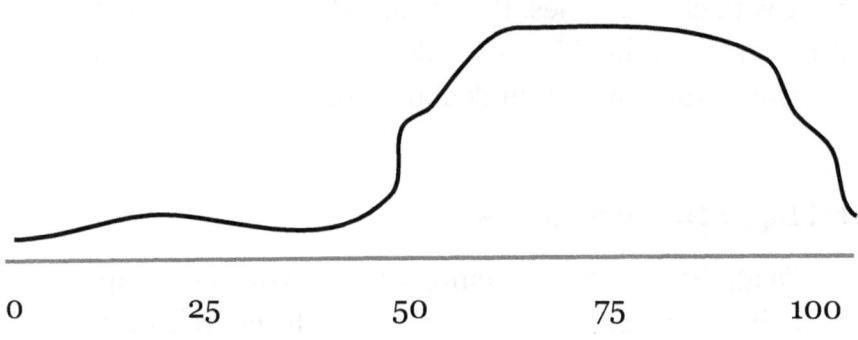

Red

The number of people in the 50+ group is twice as large as those below 50.

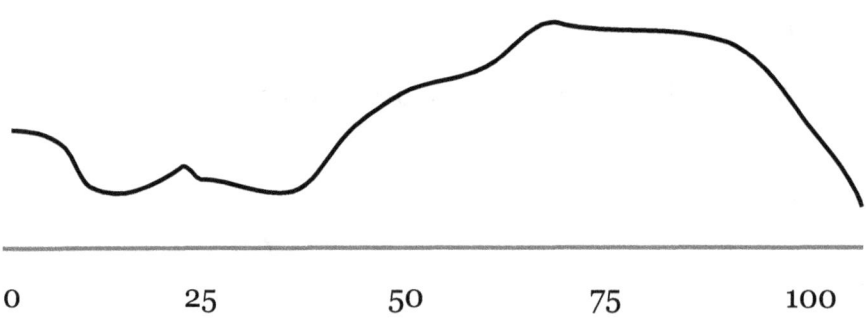

Yellow

The number of people is relatively consistent across all age levels.

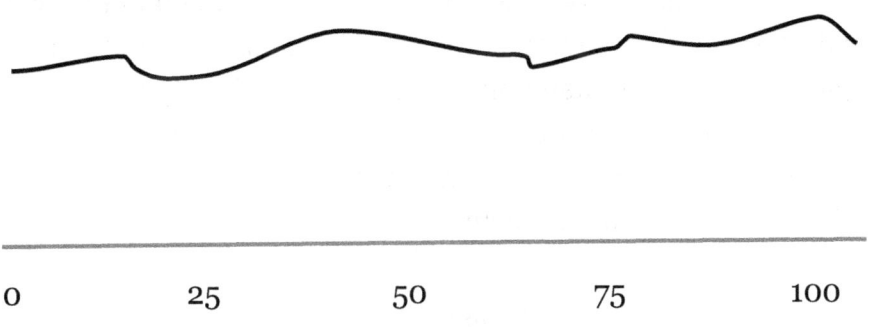

0   25   50   75   100

Green

The number of people under 50 is significantly higher than those older than 50.

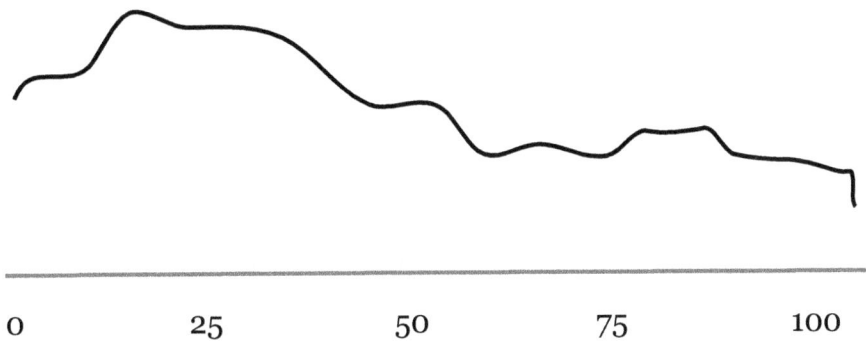

0   25   50   75   100

Vital Sign: Attendance

The next vital sign is Attendance and it can be thought of as the blood pressure of the church. In a human body, the amount of blood circulating depends on the size of the body. For a church, the number of people attending is related to the size of the community it serves and the facilities it is utilizing. This means that a congregation in a very small village, meeting in a tiny building, may have good attendance numbers that are very small. To keep things simple, we are going to use the building capacity number vs. member attendance as an indicator of healthy numbers. So for example if the building seats 120 and currently has 24 people attending the percentage would be 24/120= 0.2 or twenty percent.

The number of people in the church building every week is what percentage of its maximum capacity?

>Black: Less than 10%

>Blue: Between 10% and 20%

>Red: Between 20% and 50%

>Yellow: Between 50% and 80%

>Green: More than 80%

Vital Sign: Conversion

The final vital sign is conversion and it can be thought of as the respiratory rate of the church. Just as the human body needs to breathe in order to live, healthy churches need to welcome new converts to the faith. Clearly, a congregation that has had no new conversions for many years is revealing something about the spiritual state of the church, not to mention long term viability. It is essential for proper spiritual growth and discipleship to be taking place in the church and this vital sign gives some insight on whether or not this is happening.

The pastors in most churches will be able to estimate quite easily how many people have come to faith and can indicate what the total number is to church members. Depending on the practice of your church, you may be able to use baptisms or confirmations as an indication of conversion. Note make sure that the conversion numbers you use do not include people who only came to church for a short time and left, but ones who have become longer term contributing members of the congregation.

Number of conversions that have taken place in the church is:

Black: none for a decade

Blue: none in the last few years

Red: a few every year or so

Yellow: some every year

Green: over 10 a year

Calculate your church's score

Rate your church for each of the three church vital signs. Give yourself 1 point for Black, 2 for Blue, 3 for Red, 4 for Yellow and 5 for Green. Total the three numbers you get and divide by three and then round the result up.

For example, say you have the following: Your demographics is black = 1, attendance is red = 3 and conversion is also red = 3.

1+3+3=7 divided by 3 is 2.33 and rounded up is 3. This puts the church evaluated in the red category. The good news is this church is worth trying to save, the bad news is that it is going to take a major effort and intervention.

There are other factors to consider which we are not using, but these ones should provide you with a rough estimate of where your church is situated. Hopefully it will prevent us from fooling ourselves into thinking that things are not that bad, when in reality the situation is serious.

For most churches it will be accurate within one priority level. It is possible that you have calculated your church as a blue, but the correct evaluation really is red. At the same time, it is very possible that the level you have calculated is the correct one, but it is difficult to accept. I leave this for you to think about.

Generating the Urgency to Change

The goal of the numbers and examining the extent of the problem is not to make us all depressed, but to generate enough pain so as to overcome our tendency to remain in a state of inertia. As humans, change is typically painful because it forces us to do things differently. In our churches, people must see that the pain of not changing will be greater than the pain of changing.

It is only by fully exploring the reality of the situation before us, that we will be informed enough to stay the course of change when everything in us wants to turn back. We must realize in our heart of hearts that there is no safe harbour behind us we can find refuge in. Our only hope is to go forward into the unknown.

So how do you do this in your church? A good starting point might be to present to the congregation some of the information covered in this chapter, working out together exactly where your church falls in the church health scale and helping everyone get an accurate representation of exactly where the church currently is. It might then be appropriate to show graphically where the church will be in a few years if nothing changes.

This must not be a one-time thing that people hear once and never hear again. It is important for people to realize that the reason for the exercise is to gain an accurate representation of the situation, and this may take some time. It takes time for people to accept the reality of a bad situation and the congregation must be given time to adjust to the new reality.

There is a danger at this point, for those leading change, to want to move on too quickly to talking about the specific issues in society that have led to the current situation. They should be encouraged to wait, to make sure the message has really sunk in. It is the reality of a particular church's situation that will provide the foundation for real change. Urgency is created as we acknowledge together the problems before us. Without a sense of urgency, nothing happens.

Chapter 4 - New Market

Summary

Only God will enable a congregation to make it across the chasm that exists between the church world and normal society. Society has become so secularized that it is as if the message of Jesus is being introduced for the very first time. It is like entering a new market with the radical message of Christ. In this new market, we should expect to encounter early adopters who want to try new things, a suspicious majority who needs to be convinced, and stubborn laggards who will resist change to the bitter end. Innovative new products face an additional challenge, which is a large gap between early adopters and the majority. Christianity faces this same challenge, but it must also deal with those in the traditional church who want to stay in the past. The best way to overcome this resistance to change is to have a series of small successes before trying to make big changes.

The Gap

So is there any hope of bridging the gap between the church and society? Can the chasm be crossed? As I think about this, I am reminded of the image that is often used to portray how becoming a Christian reconnects us with God. Often the cross is represented as a bridge that lets people cross over to where God is. We are no longer separated from God because we trust in what Christ has done to achieve our salvation.

The situation is the same here. We must trust in the power of God to bridge the gap between the church and society. Just like Paul in 1 Corinthians 2:4, we must depend not on human wisdom, but on the Spirit's power. It takes God to deal with sin and it takes God to deal with this gap. At the same time, we must walk over to the other side. This will require us to put one foot ahead of the other. Learning in more detail what has happened and how we can respond, is like moving our feet across the bridge.

Now, there are some who might object to us using marketing language to describe how we can reach others with the gospel. It is true we need to be cautious not to overemphasize natural methods and forget that it is God's work to bring about the heart change. At the same time, it would be foolish not to utilize tools that can help us understand how to reach people with the good news of Christ. Just as the Apostle Paul committed himself to do everything possible to spread the gospel of Jesus, so should we.

New Market

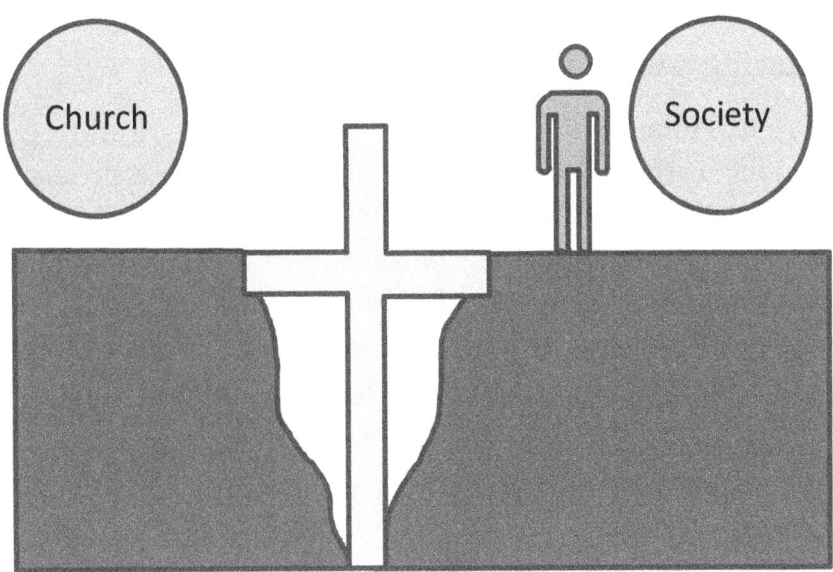

The gospel has been completely lost in society as a whole and even in the church it is often obscured. This means we must first make sure that local churches understand and are practicing the true gospel, and then reintroduce the message of Jesus back into the society as a whole.

Entering a new Market

It is important to keep in mind as well that we are introducing the message of Jesus into what business people call 'a new market'. Most people in society are aware that the Christian church exists, they have, after all, seen the buildings. A few have something against the church because of a past personal experience, but the majority have no strong opinion because, quite simply, they do not know anything about it.

This means that efforts churches make to call people back to the roots of the Christian faith are doomed to fail. You cannot call someone back to something they never had. We must approach others with the attitude that we have a foreign message that must be translated before it can be understood by modern ears. We are entering a new market and the onus is on us to explain clearly the benefits of a life committed to Jesus.

When entering a new market, it is helpful to think of the people you are trying to convert to your product, or in this case, faith, in terms of how a population adopts new ideas and products. One of the ways to represent this adoption pattern has been to divide segments of the population using a bell curve and what particular standard deviation from the mean they happen to fall in.

New Market

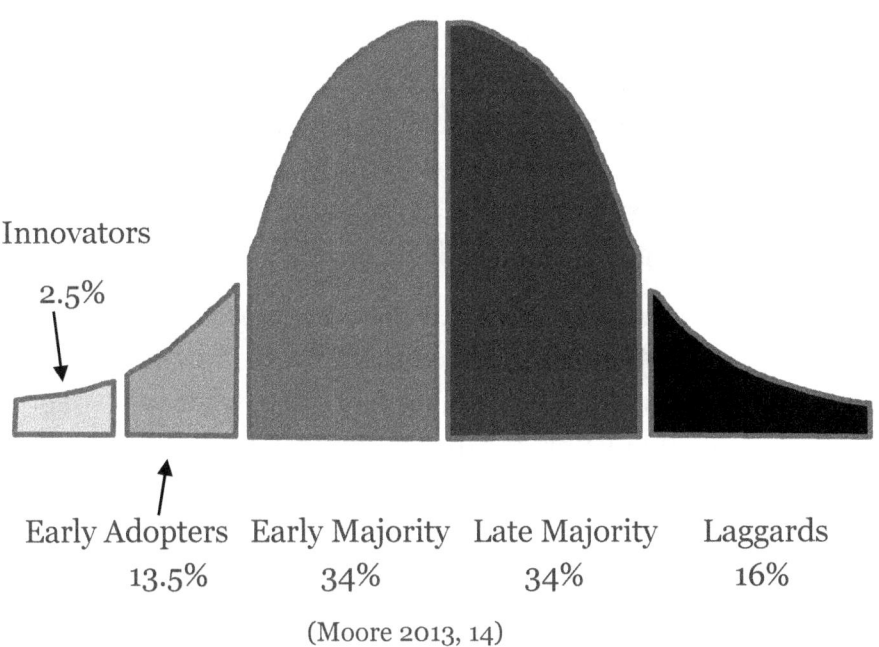

(Moore 2013, 14)

Innovators (Enthusiasts) pursue new experiences aggressively. They want to always be a part of what is happening next. When the church had the corner on the religious market in the West, these would tend to be the people pushing the envelope of spirituality. They would see themselves as forward thinking while the church would often, although not always, label them as heretics. Now that the church is in a precipitous decline in the West, these are often the people trying to point the way back to authentic Christianity. To be certain, they do not always get it right, but at least they are trying. Real authentic change will often start with these kinds of people because they are not afraid to go against the flow.

Early Adopters (Visionaries) buy into a product or service early on because they can see the vision of what might be possible. They are not the originators of the new ideas, as they depend on the innovators for that function, but they quickly become champions for the new way. They buy more into the vision than the particular product. For them it is more about what might be, than what it currently is. In our churches, many of those who are still attending regularly, even in dying churches, have the potential to be early adopters. Many still have memories of a better time and they are just waiting for someone to paint a clear vision for them to follow.

Early Majority (Pragmatists) will only buy into something when it becomes practical. Do not try and sell them a vision; they are not interested. They want to see feet on the ground and dollars in the bank before they will commit to anything. If what you are selling works, they are very, very interested, if not, then move along please. They know that many things are just passing fads and will quickly flame out, so until something proves itself, they will remain on the sidelines. Most of these people have not attended churches, because they are not convinced the church would have anything practical to offer.

Late Majority (Conservatives) are only interested in something when society says this is the standard. Like the early majority, they want things to be practical, but in addition, they want a clear indication of who the market leader is. It is not enough for something to work, but the majority must agree that it works before they will come on board. Because society has judged the Christian church to be irrelevant, this group has little interest in participating in a life of faith.

Laggards (Skeptics) are not interested in changing at all. They are happy with the way things are and see no reason to do things differently. They do not care that something new is more practical or that everyone else is using it. For as long as possible, they will continue to use the products that are familiar to them, excluding all other usurpers. There are many laggards outside of the church, but a portion of them are still hanging around churches as well. They often can become a real thorn in the side of anyone suggesting that perhaps we ought to change the way we worship in order to become more relevant.

The Innovation Gap

One thing that must be kept in mind about the adoption curve we have been looking at, is that it works best with products that are marginal improvements on previous ones. It does not work as well with products that are truly innovative and that bring disruption to the market place.

Products that are groundbreaking and life-altering face additional challenges. These issues were first identified with technology products that really disturbed the status quo. No longer does the curve stay smooth, but a large gap appears between the Early Adopter group (Visionaries) and the Early Majority group (Pragmatists).

The chasm represents the difficulty an innovative product will have being accepted by the pragmatists (early majority), despite the fact that the visionaries (early adopters) are already on board. The pragmatists, or early majority, prefer iterative improvements and do not trust disruptive innovation.

New Market

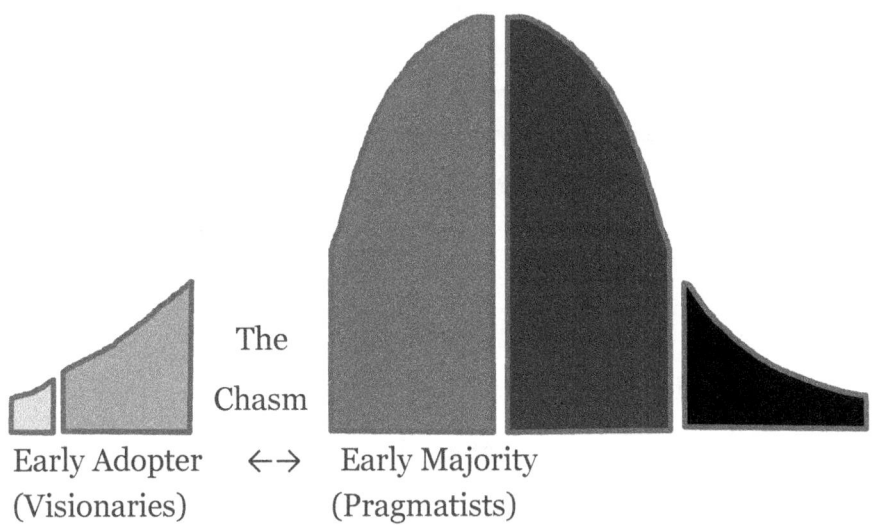

Christianity, in its true form, is most certainly a disruptive religious innovation. This is not a tough thing for early adopters to swallow because they are looking at the vision of what might be, but the early majority are not going to get on board until it becomes more practical and other practical people like themselves start participating in the market.

The gap between these visionaries in the church and the practical ones in society has always existed since Christianity began. What is unique today is that other factors have caused the innovation gap to widen into a vast chasm between church and society. Later, we will talk about five seismic shifts that have caused this, but before the chasm can be dealt with, it is critical to talk about how an older product can work against the introduction of a new one.

The Pull of the Past

Christianity in the West can be thought of as a new product because in many ways it is. It has all of the disadvantages of trying to bring a new product to market. At the same time, it has the additional disadvantage of having a segment of laggards/skeptics who actively fight against change. This makes it critical that the early adopter segment of a church is completely sold on a new vision and is of sufficient size to stand up to the skeptics before any substantive action takes place.

New Market

Traditional Church   New Church

                  Church gap   The
                      ↓   Chasm

Laggards   Early Adopters
(Skeptics)   (Visionaries)

Most churches trying to implement the changes necessary to bridge the chasm and connect to normal people in society, will have to deal with a backlash from skeptics who want to keep the church following outdated traditions. They want to continue to experience the product they are used to and will attempt to pull the church back to the past if they see change happening.

It is important not to see these people as the enemy, but as people who became attached to a particular church product and do not want to see it changed. Change is tough and they need all of our sympathy and support, but at the same time, we must continue to proclaim the message that only a changed church can ever hope to reach typical people.

Reaching consensus

It is absolutely critical that the church reaches a consensus on what it is trying to achieve. The challenge of bridging the chasm is too big a task not to have a solid majority fully committed to it. The rule would be: 'Not everyone, but most everyone.'

So how do you bring this about in your church? If, after presenting the compelling evidence that change must happen, there is still a significant fraction of church members who do not want to move forward, you must go for the easy wins. Now is not the time to begin talking too much about the seismic shifts; planning for big changes is definitely off the table. Your goal is to convert more of those in the skeptic group and bring them over to the visionary side. If you are able to bring a laggard into the visionary camp it can be like a dam breaking in its effect on the spiritual life of the congregation. For this to happen you must start with some successes.

Pick something that you believe is achievable, no matter how small it is. What is critical is that it is something you know can happen. For example, a good goal for the small church I attended last Sunday would be to get the windows cleaned so you can actually see out of them. Each new goal is introduced as an experiment with the words, "We are going to try this for blank amount of time and then evaluate the results." If it does not work, you celebrate the fact you found out what not to do. If it does work, you celebrate what has been done and potentially commit to doing it on an ongoing basis.

After a time, the skeptics will either convert to visionaries or they may make a last ditch attempt to stop the entire process. When this fails, be prepared for many of them to leave. At this point, you are ready to move on to the next steps in the process.

Chapter 5 - Preparing Minds

Summary

    In order to have spiritual transformation take place we must have a proper mental mindset. We must focus on the positive because ultimately, only this will bring about real change. People deal very poorly with a negative vision and will often ignore it and refuse to change. We must place a positive vision before the people and encourage people to dream about what might be. This vision of a preferred future is the catalyst for bringing it about. At the same time, leaders must be careful not to try and cast too wide a vision and thereby lose focus. Doing one thing well, instead of three poorly, should be our motto. A faster development timeline is essential to find out what works and feedback from your actual target market will provide this. Through it all, the people will remain on course if, and only if, the vision has embedded itself deeply in their souls.

Mental tools

We have identified that spiritual transformation must take place in the people; That a congregation must be healthy enough to make changes and that there must be a commitment on the part of the members to move forward. There is one last task, which is to prepare ourselves with the kinds of mental tools we will need to make the crossing, before we go into more detail about the seismic shifts.

Through all of this process, we must keep in mind that we are breaking into a new market with an innovative product. Because our product is life-changing, it will naturally encounter resistance. We must have the proper systems in place to channel this criticism into new and more effective programs.

Note the resistance here is from secular people in society, not from those in the church. As was already indicated, if you do not have more members who want to move forward, compared to those who do not, then you can do nothing. At that point, you need to put all energy as a church into changing that reality, before any other change or modification can even be considered.

Stay Positive

It is an interesting fact that people are led by a positive vision and will ignore a negative one. I read once about a classroom of kids that had both types of vision presented to them. There had been the typical amount of garbage accumulating in the classroom during the day. First, the negative vision was presented with teachers lecturing the students on the importance of putting garbage in the garbage can. This was met with some resistance and very little change. Next, a positive vision was tried. Despite the fact that the classroom had not changed in tidiness, teachers began to comment that this classroom was one of the cleanest classrooms in the school. Very shortly, the classroom became very tidy. The positive vision that the teachers presented was what the students worked to produce. The old saying, "You catch more flies with honey than you do with vinegar," comes to mind.

We do not have to lie to get this effect. In most situations, if we look hard, we can find something positive to comment about. That is where we should start, not with how people are falling short and not measuring up to the mark. I remember being in a church where 20 minutes of the sermon was taken up with how the congregation needed to shape up, with only the last three minutes providing any positive message at all.

We most definitely need to hear the truth about sin, but if that is the main focus, we are in trouble. Based purely on a physiological basis, this methodology will not work. Our brains tend to tune out negative and threatening messages and real change in people is blocked. Communicating with people in this way triggers defense mechanisms and diminishes their capacity to adapt. If we want people to experience real and sustained change, this is not the right path. This was explained on page 70 of *Coaching for Change:*

To summarize, arousal of the PEA (Positive Emotional Attractor) helps a person prepare for and engage in sustained, desired change. Arousal of the NEA (Negative Emotional Attractor) does the opposite. It facilitates a person closing down and avoiding anything that might induce more stress. It is a defensive posture and invokes diminished capacity for adaptation because it is following an instinctive physiological reaction to chronic or acute prolonged stress to protect the organism (Boyatzis 2010, 70).

Imagine a church that wants to experience revival. One of the worst things the people can do is only focus on all of the issues and problems. It is true that if the roof of the church is leaking, this is a major issue, and not being able to meet the budget is a big problem, but if problems become their only focus, substantive change and revival will not occur.

Place a vision before the people

A positive vision is a key piece of the puzzle that allows people to begin shifting toward a better future and real change in the church. This vision is not a "close our eyes and pray God will get us out of this mess" mentality. It is an open-eyed realistic vision of what could be; believing that what is possible is not limited by our own strength, but depends on what the Spirit of God could do among us. In their book *Pathway to Renewal*, Smith and Sellon say:

> Then, having developed a new perspective on congregational life, they dream about shifts that

renewal would bring if those peak moments were the norm. They project the difference that renewal would make for themselves and for those beyond the congregation's doors (Smith and Sellon, p. 79).

Leaders have the job of helping congregations come to the point where they can begin to imagine a preferred future. Note that this is not based on unrealistic expectations, but as the quote infers, on the peak moments the congregation has experienced in the past. It is the job of leaders to help congregations see what might be possible if they are directed by the Spirit of God.

At the same time, leaders must be careful not to allow the people to fall into the trap of following them instead of God. It is an easy trap to fall into when, in the minds of the members of the congregation, the line between what the leader is doing and what God is doing is sometimes fuzzy. It is critical that leaders direct the people to follow the vision that God has given the group.

A vision that comes from the very heart of God and has caught fire in the hearts of the people is the goal. It is this positive vision that will enable people to be substantively changed in their thinking. An excellent example of this is the powerful vision that Paul presents in Ephesians 3:14-19:

> [14] For this reason I kneel before the Father, [15] from whom every family[a] in heaven and on earth derives its name. [16] I pray that out of his glorious riches he may strengthen you with power through his Spirit in your inner being, [17] so that Christ may dwell in your hearts through faith. And I pray that

you, being rooted and established in love, [18] may have power, together with all the Lord's holy people, to grasp how wide and long and high and deep is the love of Christ, [19] and to know this love that surpasses knowledge—that you may be filled to the measure of all the fullness of God.

Focus on a beachhead

The ultimate goal is to have the love and mercy of God permeate all of society, not in a way that brings about a second Christendom (where the power of the church reaches into the political arena) like in the Middle Ages, but in a way that changes people by choice, not by force. In order for that longer-term goal to occur, churches must first establish beachheads on the mainland of society. We must stop trying to maintain the status quo on our tiny Christian island that is slipping into the sea.

This beachhead is one small area into which we can pour all of our resources and become the leader in that one specific area. We must dominate that one segment of the beach. Opposition forces will not take kindly to us invading their turf, so we must be prepared to fight with all of the love, mercy and compassion that God can pour into us. Just as the Allied forces fought hard to take the beaches of Normandy from the Axis powers, so we, as the church, must fight for our beach. Later, the task of breaking out and freeing more occupied territory can be contemplated, but if we do not take the beach, it is all for naught.

Many churches spread their resources too thin, trying to do too many things. It is infinitely better to do a few things well. In the current situation where we find ourselves, we have no other choice.

Rapid Development

In a number of ways, time is an enemy for the church. In the first place, for many churches, the average age of the congregants is so high, there is a limited amount time for a turnaround to occur. Secondly, there are only so many resources, and there is a danger they could run out before the breakthrough occurs. Thirdly, if some level of success does not occur quickly, the segment in the church who did not want change in the first place may obtain enough support to stop the process entirely.

Given that time is not our friend, we must change how quickly we develop, implement and evaluate programs. Speed of change must shift from years to months and in some cases, even weeks. Our new motto must become "Attempt, evaluate, attempt, evaluate..." Make a change and evaluate its effectiveness, adjust our target and try again.

The first step is to identify a key learning goal or metric that you want to achieve. Once this is identified, do the smallest thing possible to test a falsifiable hypothesis. The test should only change one factor and be specific and testable (Mauyra 2012, 29%). If your test is vague you can fool yourself into believing what you hope to be true. Your goal is, as quickly as possible, to find out that what you thought might be true is actually wrong.

This means you must test your hypothesis on the actual people you want to reach, not on your current church attenders.

How this works in practice is quite simple. Let us say that a part of the church membership wants to replace the aging carpet with new tile, but another group wants to keep the carpet as they believe it has a few good years left. Typically in churches, this would come down to the two groups fighting for what they want. If, however, the church has identified that they are committed to reaching the surrounding community, then the opinions of both groups are irrelevant. What is needed is the smallest possible test to see if the switch to tile will actually make a difference for the target group. The church members decide that the opinion of five non-church members is enough to test if tile is better than carpet. Five people from outside the church are brought in for a five minute look at the carpet and the possible new tile. They agree that tile is better, but suggest that the church might want to consider a different style of tile other than the one currently selected. Now, new tests can be formulated on the basis of evidence obtained from your target market, instead of member conjecture and personal preference.

Focused Vision

It is important, before you really start tackling the seismic shifts in your congregation, that everyone understands how to implement effective change. Church members and leaders may need some training on exactly how this works. Leaders, in particular, may need practice in presenting a positive vision of the future instead of highlighting failures of the past. Church members may need to adjust to the speed at which rapid development takes place; embracing change instead of holding on to the past. Everyone must come to terms with the reality that priorities must be implemented. The hardest choices are not the things you do, but the things you choose not to do for the sake of expediency and focus.

The question raised at this point might be, why do we have to focus on a few things? Can't we keep doing the things we have already been doing and just add a few more things?

The reason it is important to be so focused and only implement those things that are in line with your vision, is because of the Innovation Gap. Remember that every disruptive innovation will always struggle to get a foothold in the early majority or pragmatic market segment. It is only as these people see you doing something really well that they will consider the possibility of engaging with you.

The Innovation Gap requires that we generate trust in the group we are trying to reach by focusing on being excellent in one area. Yes, it is possible to do more than just one thing well, but there is a danger of becoming scattered in our approach. Too many churches try to be all things to all people and do nothing well. The Innovation Gap requires more from us than this. It requires a positive vision that is focused on achieving excellence in a narrow area.

This vision must become something the church has agreed on, without being coerced. The vision provides the blueprint of what you are trying to build and even more importantly, clarifies what you are not building. It is only a vision that has embedded itself deeply into the soul of the people that will sustain a church as it attempts to cross the chasm.

A Chasm Crossing Church

78

Part 2

The Five Seismic Shifts

There was a time in the Western world, during the Middle Ages, when there was no separation between the church and society. The church had a primary role in shaping and being involved in culture. The church did not always operate in appropriate ways, but few questioned the legitimacy of it being involved in society. This era of Christendom was certainly more political than it should have been, but at its core, the gospel message of Jesus was still very much present.

This situation can be represented by a solid landmass with the church taking up a significant chunk of the social scene.

Since that time, there have been seismic shifts that have caused a separation between the church and the rest of society and these have been unique in human history. It is true that societies in the past experienced shifts that caused them to change drastically. One can think of wars, plagues and invasions that have had a huge impact on the social framework of nations. What makes this situation so different is the new mechanisms by which changes take place.

These five seismic shifts have moved the church and normal society so far apart that we are now in a situation where much of Western society experiences very little Christian influence. This has been a huge change and its significance cannot be understated.

Chapter 6 - Modern Science

Summary

The first seismic shift between the church and the rest of society was Modern Science. Science, as we know it, was only able to come into existence because of Christian theology (Stark 2004, 123). Even today it still contains, at its core, a set of Christian philosophical assumptions. As the scientific revolution gathered steam, anti-Christian intellectuals spread the lie that science had proven Christianity to be false, when in fact, it did no such thing.

Science provides us great insight into the natural world, but tells us nothing about the spiritual one. Science has also clarified some things we read about in the Bible, but in no way should we allow it to be the only acceptable authority. Both Christianity and Science have very valuable things to say. Modern people have a science mindset and they expect to see practical results in our churches. They have a discovery mentality that wants to know the answers to how things work. They are comfortable when we test things to see what works and change our traditions when they are no longer appropriate. We need to hold firm to the truth of the unchanging gospel, while we make adjustments to the methods used to convey it.

1st seismic shift: Modern Science

The first seismic shift that created a gap between the church and the rest of Western Society was Modern Science. Science provided reasons for physical processes that had traditionally been considered to be within the bounds of church authority. Of all of the seismic shifts, this one took the longest and was the most traumatic. This makes sense when you think about the fact that the end result was a tearing apart of the church from the rest of society. This fact was even codified by some countries as the separation of church and state. At this point, people still considered the church to be very important; although there was a gap, the distance was not very far. Here is a picture of this situation.

The Rise of Science

At its core, science has a core set of philosophical assumptions. These values guide how work is to be done, if it is to be done scientifically. These assumptions do not come from science itself, nor can they be proven by it. They must be accepted on faith. The first of these assumptions is that order exists in nature. A universe that provides random results to the same initial test conditions could not sustain the scientific enterprise, so we ignore this possibility. Secondly, we are capable of observing the order that is inherent in nature. If our powers of observation were faulty, there would be no hope to discover anything, since our senses could deceive us, so we ignore this as well. Thirdly, it is possible to derive models that will provide naturalistic explanations for the phenomena we have observed and enable us to predict future results. If there was not an inherent logicalness to the universe, this would not be possible and so this is ignored (Peters, 31).

Put in other words, we believe that if we repeat a natural experiment the results will be the same the next time. We believe we have the power to understand correctly what we see. We believe that we can use logic to create models that will predict how future projects and experiments will turn out.

It may be difficult for someone who has been raised in Western culture to understand just how strange these assumptions actually are. They are by no means logical or natural and cannot be proven. In this sense, science is a faith-based exercise. We assume there is a true and objective reality that exists outside of our immediate perceptions. We assume that we are not insane and have the capability to comprehend it. We assume that reality is not the product of our own minds. We assume the world could have been different, but that it is the result of particular causes to make it the way it is (Wilcox, 11).

For most of recorded history, people have not thought like this. In most cultures that have existed, to have this kind of faith would have been dangerous and perhaps even life-ending. Even today, some major Eastern religions consider physical reality an illusion. In order for Modern Science to be born and then flourish, it needed an environment of belief and faith that would nourish it. This occurred for the first time ever in Christian Europe during the Middle Ages. This was put well by Rodney Stark in *The Victory of Reason*.

> The Christian image of God is that of a rational being who believes in human progress, more fully revealing himself as humans gain the capacity to better understand. Moreover, because God is a rational being and the universe is his personal creation, it necessarily has a rational, lawful, stable structure, awaiting increased human comprehension. This was the key to many intellectual undertakings, among them the rise of science (Stark 2007, 7%).

All the other cultures have had religious and philosophical doctrines that placed insurmountable barriers in front of scientific faith, except for Christianity. Faithful believers in Christ were encouraged by the church to investigate God's creation. They developed science because they believed not only that could it be done, but that it should be done.

Later on, in what is called the Age of Enlightenment, some intellectuals propagated the lie that science was victorious over a Church that was oppressive and anti-science. They were somewhat successful in obscuring the importance of Christianity in the rise of science, but the historical evidence tells a different story. The reality is that science is the product of Christianity. Faith in science is not opposed to faith in Christ, but is actually dependent on Christianity for its existence. Those who participated in the scientific achievements of the sixteenth and seventeenth centuries saw themselves as pursuing the secrets of God's creation (Stark 2007, 8%).

Not only was science dependent on Christianity to develop, but even today, it shares an underlying philosophical outlook with it. This is despite the fact that some critics of Christianity have done their best to create a new philosophical foundation for science based on what they call natural religion (Brooke, 163). Elements of this can be seen in the religious pluralism that is currently in fashion in the West.

At their core, Christianity and Science are not only compatible, but actually part of the same faith family. Modern science, despite all protests to the contrary, is the daughter of a Christian mother. One seeks the truth in the spiritual realm, while the other seeks truth in the natural one, but both operate by faith. A faith that is at its core fundamentally Christian.

What Science has achieved and what it cannot do

While it is true that there have been times the Christian church has opposed scientific findings that it felt were at odds with spiritual truths found in scripture, it is important to remember that science exists because of Christian thinking. When Nicolaus Copernicus proposed a new heliocentric model of the solar system, is was predicated on the works of many others who had been educated at Christian universities. What he brought about was not the start of a revolution, but the logical next step in an ongoing search for truth in the natural world by Christians (Stark 2007, 22%).

As Christians figured out how to use technology to create better tools (like the telescope), they were able to use the scientific method to discover ways to make even better tools. These improved tools then facilitated better science and so the cycle continued. Better microscopes revealed a new world of tiny organisms. This information allowed scientists to understand, for the first time, how certain types of pathogens spread in the human population. The fantastic discovery of penicillin to fight bacterial infection occurred because of research into microorganisms. My mother would have died as a girl from spinal meningitis, except for the radical new step of administering large doses of antibiotics.

Modern Science, undertaken by those who themselves may not be Christians, but who operate from a Christian Philosophical position, has brought us many wonderful things. It has also revealed some things that are at odds with the traditional Christian Church explanation of particular natural events. Two things are important to note: First, these discoveries do not impact the fundamentals of the Christian Faith. Secondly, the Church has had a number of different opinions regarding different events in the natural world and some of these match up amazingly well with what has been discovered.

Now, there are those who argue that science has shown that Christianity is false. They have stated that miracles are not supernatural, but are just improbable natural events (Dawkins,

139). This is not proof at all, but just a circular argument. For these people, the Christian understanding of a consistent universe has become so ingrained; they cannot see that what they are saying is actually a faith statement.

In reaction to these attacks, I understand very well why there were those in the church who retreated behind religious walls and proclaimed that all of the scientists were wrong. They perceived correctly that science was being used to attack the church, but failed to comprehend that it was simply a tool being used by those who wanted to malign the Church. Science is not the enemy, but was co-opted by those who desired to destroy Christianity.

It is not a matter of choosing the Bible or choosing science; the two are compatible in a wonderful way. Together, they can be a powerful weapon to fight those whose purpose is to get rid of God. To do this, we must drop the idea that we understand everything in the Bible perfectly. This does not reduce the truth of scripture one iota, but introduces the fact that perhaps our human understanding is not all-encompassing. We need to welcome the fact that science sheds new light on stories from the bible, while at the same time remembering that Scripture can help keep science from getting off track.

Science and the Bible

At the very beginning of the Bible, we read that God created the universe out of nothing. As Christians, we inherited the belief from Judaism that this actually happened. Consider for a moment how strange this is. Nothing becomes something. That is crazy. Most other religions and cultures came up with the idea that what is has always been, or what we see is illusion or some convoluted tale of multiple creations of things by a pantheon of gods. To believe that all that is came from nothing borders on the incredulous, but this is what Christians believed by faith.

Along comes science and it is able to demonstrate that Christianity is right. According to the big bang theory, the entire universe was created from nothing, a tiny point that exploded into the vastness of the universe. For faith traditions like Christianity that describe the universe as being created by God from nothingness, this is absolutely amazing (Collins, 66).

The next question logically would be, but doesn't Christianity teach that the world was created in literal days? It is true that at the present time there are Christians who believe this, but today and down through history, there have been many different Christian interpretations regarding how long the process took. The reason that there could be different interpretations is that it is not fundamental to the Christian faith. It was a peripheral idea and not part of the core beliefs that all Christians agreed on.

In Christian history, there have been those who have argued for long periods of time. They pointed out, quite correctly, that the Hebrew word used in Genesis 1 for day (yôm) can be used to refer to time periods or ages. There are places in the Bible where yôm is used in a nonliteral context, such as "the day of the Lord". Even in the English language today, despite that fact that typically a day means 24 hours, often we use the word to define shorter or much longer periods of time. For example: "How was your day at work?" or "Every dog has its day" (Collins, 152). Other Christians argued that the timeline was very short and some even thought creation happened in six literal days.

The debate in Christianity between those who said the process took a short period of time and others who said it was a long period of time, is over. Science has shown that it happened over a very long period of time. Instead of negating the Christian faith, this discovery actually clarifies it. It is nice to now know which of the lines of Christian thinking was correct.

Another area that Christianity and Science agree on is Adam. The Bible says that after all of the other plants and animals were created, a special human was created who was called Adam. Science has proven this to be correct. All people are the result of one individual who experienced a chromosome fusion (Wilcox, 132). The Bible tells us that he would interact with his environment in a new way and would subdue the earth. Paleontology has found evidence of this starting to happen, as humans became the first creatures to use tools.

The Bible says there was something very special about this creature; that he was made in the image of God. Science cannot measure the spiritual dimension of humans, but there is evidence for this specialty. DNA analysis has shown that we are part of one family with remarkably low genetic diversity. This distinguishes us from most other species on the planet (Collins, 126). This dovetails nicely with the truth that Christianity has always taught, namely that we are all the same as humans and no one is any higher or lower than any other.

Christianity and Science in proper perspective

There are still parts of the Bible that we do not fully understand, just as there are things in nature that are beyond us. The fact that science cannot explain all natural processes does not mean we need to throw out science. It means we need to keep looking. The fact that Christianity cannot fully explain all of the spiritual things does not mean we should throw it out either. We need to keep praying and inquiring.

When Science and Christianity seem to be in conflict, it would be better to say we do not know what happened. This does not prove Science wrong and neither does it prove Christianity wrong. An example of jumping to conclusions is an argument that critics of Christianity have used in the past. They said that since, in Genesis, it says that God created light first, then separated it from darkness and only later created the heavenly bodies, this proved, according to them, that the Bible is false, because suns are required to produce light. Obviously the scripture is wrong, but wait. According to the new Big Bang theory, this is exactly what happened.

There was a blinding flash of light, then a dark period and only later did the suns appear.

Modern Science

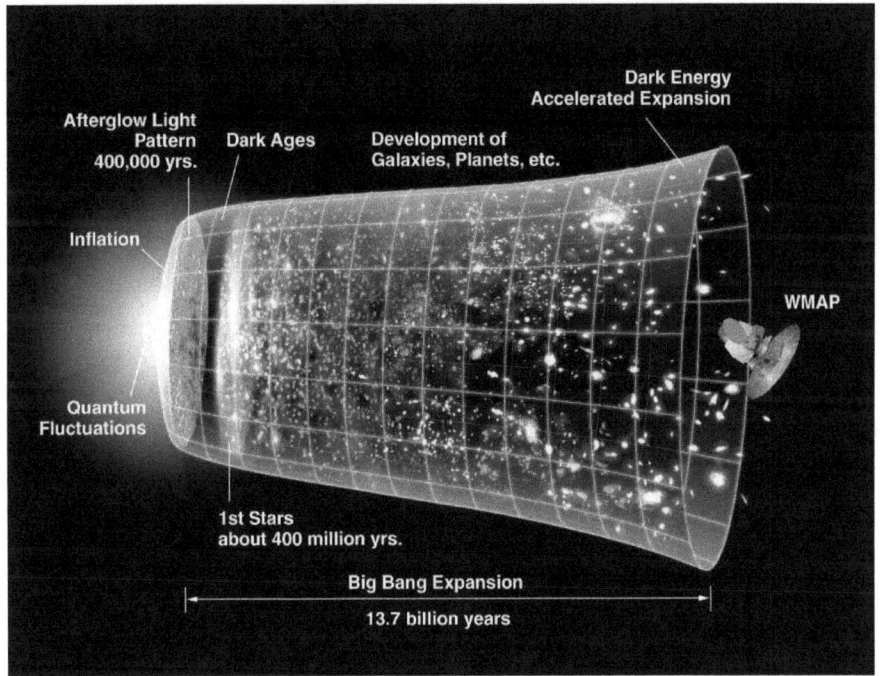

Credit: NASA / WMAP Science Team

On the far left of the picture you see the blinding flash of light. At this point in the universe (according to the theory) the only thing that existed was light. There was no darkness. Next, the light fades to total darkness called the Dark Ages and now dark has been separated from light. Finally, stars begin to form and produce light. This is a case where our understanding of science had been incomplete and now we understand it more fully. What was perceived as a contradiction between Christianity and Science has been eliminated by new scientific discoveries.

If Science is the daughter of Christianity and both of them are concerned about different areas of truth, why has there been so much conflict? The answer is that there were those who realized they could use scientific results to attack Christianity. They may have believed in other spiritual forces or been atheistic in their thinking, but the result was that science became bound up with materialism. Materialism said that all that exists is matter, which orders itself and is unguided and without purpose. Christianity is a supernatural religion that says there is a reality outside of matter and this spiritual reality provides purpose and order to the material world (Wilcox, 15).

This means that today, even good science often comes shrink-wrapped in these non-scientific ideologies like atheistic materialism (Peters, 6%). This has detached Science from its Christian spiritual roots and blinded people to the philosophical presuppositions they are making. If you say that naturally occurring phenomena are the only evidence ever allowed, you have already rendered the verdict that God does not exist before a single experiment is done (Committee, 26%).

The gap between Science and Christianity

In the 19th century, as the Western church came under fire by this kind of materialistic thinking, it reacted in two ways. Theologically liberal churches decided to accept what materialistic science said and attempted to find a place for the church to fit in with this new thinking. Typically this was done by downplaying the spiritual and focusing on social issues. Fundamentalist churches decided to ignore everything materialistic science said and live in an alternate universe. Typically this was done by holding fast to the position that only what the Bible says is true.

What this has done is open up a huge gap between Western Christianity and the rest of society. It is incumbent on the Church to close this gap by recognizing that, fundamentally, Science and Christianity are compatible, while at the same time taking a stand against materialistic atheism, an Atheism that has co-opted the scientific method in its efforts to destroy Christianity. The scientific method can never access spiritually-based information (Kuehne, 107) and it is precisely this point that the Church must stress.

Science is a wonderful way to gather knowledge, and like a microscope, it allows us to see things that have been hidden from us in the past, but if we only ever look through a microscope lens and never go back to looking at things with our normal eyes, we will be in serious trouble.

Connecting to the Science Mind

In many congregations that are declining, the main stumbling block to renewal is not the level of prayer and commitment, but an unwillingness to change how things are done. Old traditions have become a spiritually deadening blanket that snuffs out the fire of God. These traditions have become idols and are stopping people from following Jesus.

This kind of traditional thinking is anathema to those who have a science mindset. A scientist follows particular rules and theories, but is always looking for evidence that points the way to new knowledge. Good scientists even create specific experiments to try and prove that the way things have always been understood or done are incorrect. Normal people in Western society have a primarily scientific mindset. This is not to say that they run complicated experiments, but that they agree with the scientific way of doing things. They may not like to change, but if a new truth is discovered, most people will accept it and begin integrating this new knowledge into their understanding of the world.

People today want to see practical results and they are comfortable with trying and testing new things to see if these will achieve what they are looking for. They are goal-orientated in their thinking and above all, they want to see progress. For them, change is not a bad word, but a necessary element in discovering what works and what is true.

Our churches must free themselves from the bindings of "This is the way it has always been." We must evaluate our traditions based on their purpose and if it is being achieved. Holding on to the methodologies of the past, out of nostalgia, is not going to cut it in the modern world and will not help us deal with the Chasm.

The question might be asked, "How do I change the minds of people in my congregation who are stuck in the past and absolutely refuse to change?" The answer to this is vision and results. As was talked about previously, you must have a vision that clarifies what the church is trying to achieve. The first question you must ask is, have the people bought into the vision? If this is not the case, you can forget about trying to change anything. Stop trying to start something new and go back to solidifying the vision with the congregation. If, on the other hand, the vision is honestly accepted by the members and they are committed to it, the place to start is results: running small tests for short periods of time in order to identify what is better. This will help people move to a scientific testing mindset. Once some small experiments demonstrate significant improvement, you can then bring forth the evidence that this new method is better suited to achieving the church's vision.

Traditions typically contain some very positive things and teach us some truths. The problem arises when we lose sight of why they were implemented in the first place. It may well be that some traditions are blocking the church from moving forward and these are the ones that need to die.

Because of all of this, it is quite understandable the loss people feel as traditions and rituals that they have grown up with are removed. There needs to be a place allowed for mourning and grieving that which has gone. Compassion must always be a part of the equation, but this must not prevent us from removing ineffective methods and replacing them with what works.

Chapter 7 - Productive Society

Summary

The second seismic shift between the church and society was Productive Society. New production tools increased income and living standards dramatically. The free markets that facilitated this process, to a large extent, owed their existence to Christianity. It provided the theological foundation that encouraged productivity. Inventions of all kinds were the result of the Christian hope that a better life was possible, not only in heaven to come, but in the here and now as well (Stark 2014, 22%). As time went on, runaway consumption eventually led to consumerism and the sins of self-sufficiency and pride. Now the church must address the dark side of a productive society while at the same time providing excellent customer service to a society that expects it.

2nd seismic shift: Productive Society

As a result of science and experimentation, more effective tools of production were invented. Free markets then provided a platform for goods to be exchanged in an efficient way. As a result of this, income and living standards increased dramatically for those in the West. This started with the owners of these new production tools, but over time, it trickled down to practically everyone who was a part of these societies. This seismic shift of Productive Society pulled the church and society farther apart. Here is a picture of the increased distance between the church and society:

Rise of Free Markets

Many reasons have been put forth for the rise of free markets in Christian Europe during the Middle Ages, including: merchant class, patent protections, lower taxation, geography, and the domestication of plants and animals (Diamond, 410). All of these factors played a part, but many would argue that the primary cause was Christianity.

Some would say that this occurred over a long period of time during the Middle Ages and that the Industrial Revolution was just the end result of this process (Stark 2007, 3%). Others would say that it was the rise of Protestantism and in particular Calvinistic thought that created the ideology necessary for free markets to come into existence (Weber 1992, 9).

In either case, it is clear that Christian theology has played a significant part in creating free markets where capitalistic firms compete with each other to sell goods to customers. It promoted a faith in progress and a work ethic that were essential building blocks in the creation of this new system of production and trade.

We can see some of these ideas in the New Testament. In Ephesians 3:20, Paul talks about how God is still at work within us and in Philippians 2:12, that it is our responsibility to work out our salvation in fear and trembling. It was not much of a leap to think that if we are to expect progress in the spiritual realm then progress should also occur in the natural realm. Other passages are even more clear about our responsibility to work and not be a burden on others. 2 Thessalonians 3:6-10 says that those who are not willing to work should not be allowed to eat.

It was Christian theology that gave rise to the new economic model. The Christian belief in a better future made people willing to adapt to new ideas and implement methods that promised to be improvements (Stark 2014, 22%). This was not the case in most other cultures, which often made limited use of the things they invented. For example, paper was invented in

China, but it was only in Europe that it was produced on a large scale and resulted in a print culture (Weber 1992, xxx).

The Specialization Advantage

In a free market society there are many factors that may allow one group to produce goods more cheaply than another, but one of the most important is specialization. Specialists are able to produce goods far more efficiently than non-specialists and this results in them being far cheaper. Even those less well off in a society are able to gain access to products that would be unaffordable in a non-specialized society (Butler 2011, 11).

Let us look at an example. If we approximate the cost of producing a particular product using 10 dollars an hour, then a product that takes 12 hours to produce will have a total price of $120. If, through specialization, we are able to reduce the time down to 2 hours, then the total price will be reduced to $20.

Productive Society

In the end, more people are able to afford the product at the lower cost and, as a result, more people are able to experience the benefit of owning this particular item. It is the power of specialization and the application of more efficient production tools that has resulted in the standard of living climbing in the industrialized west (Nye 2008).

Economic theory indicates that this model is beneficial economically even for the person or country that does not have a comparative advantage of production in any area (Baumol 2016, 49).

Off the Rails

Although free markets and the increased level of production that resulted from them brought benefits, this came at a cost. Some have seen this as trapping us in a system that is more concerned about efficiency than people (Weber 1992, 123). In the end, it has lead us down the road to materialism and consumerism. Over time, the material world became the only thing that mattered and the balance sheet the only thing that counted. The spiritual dimension of life was deemed as irrelevant and human needs were not considered.

Our societies have been able to create more and more things at lower and lower costs, but for many the very act of acquiring more has become an addiction. Runaway consumption has worked its way from the market place into the religious dimension of life (Bell, 21). Our Christianity has often become more concerned about how congregants feel, rather than about what God wants.

The church has struggled with how to deal effectively with materialism. It correctly ascertained that the overemphases on material things was doing damage to the hearts of the people, but it has often been muted in its response. A few in the church, like those who believe in the prosperity gospel, were even sucked into the materialistic vortex.

Our challenge now is to affirm the benefits of a productive society, while at the same time highlighting where this model has problems.

Bridging the Gap between the Church and Productive Society

The reason this seismic shift has created such a gap between society and the church is a shift in attitude toward "change" by church members. As indicated, Christianity has always been a forward-thinking religion and Christians were the first to implement new methodologies and technologies. However, as the battle between atheistic philosophers played out in the 19th and 20th centuries, the church went on the defensive and came to value consistency as a virtue. The message proclaimed was: Let the world outside change, but within the walls of the church, things will stay the same. The church lost touch with its revolutionary heart, both spiritually and materially, settling for a religion of comfort and familiarity.

Now is the time for the church to get back to being the innovator it really is, overcoming the fear of change and implementing new things that will make a substantive difference. Instead of focusing on comfort, it needs to be the first to speak out on issues of economic injustice and declare to the world that we are made for more than just economic production. At the same time, we must be willing to let go of the familiar in order to communicate the gospel in a language that modern people can understand.

Becoming Customer-Centered

As Western society gained higher and higher levels of productivity, the amount of goods available for purchase increased dramatically. Given the higher wages workers were receiving and the reduced cost of producing many items, the number of things owned by each person went way up. People began to expect and demand higher quality and variety. They were no longer stuck with limited selection and buying from sellers who held a monopoly on the market.

People in society now expect to have quality products and quality experiences. There are times in which churches have settled for second best in their programs and this cannot continue. In our congregations, we need to move from offering fixed programs to offering responsive ones, doing all that we can to include the input of those who are using our programs and services. In short, we need to provide excellent customer service.

An obvious question is, how do we encourage members of our churches to have this outlook? One of the answers is to do all we can to allow members to experience ownership of what the church is trying to accomplish and rewarding the kinds of behavior we want to see more of.

It is critical that leaders give more control to the members. The people need to know that the decisions they make matter and will not be arbitrarily overturned, otherwise they will stop investing in the process. The same can be said for a congregation that never allows its leaders to lead. A sense of ownership is critical in order for the church to change into a responsive organization.

Productive Society

Chapter 8 - Human Freedom

Summary

The third seismic shift between the church and society was Human Freedom. The modern understanding of Human Freedom arose in Christianity during the Middle Ages. It was Christian nations that became the first societies where all people were no longer slaves (not the specific property of someone else) and they started to move toward the establishment of responsible governments.

Over time, Human Freedom was taken too far. Freedom for the sake of freedom pushed out responsibility toward God and encouraged people to indulge in all kinds of behavior that harmed themselves and others. The church responded by being too lenient on some sins, like gossip, and too harsh in others and this has resulted in a gap between church people and people in society who want to experience entertainment and fun.

3rd seismic shift: Human Freedom

As new kinds of communication technology were invented, they enabled a wider broadcasting of new ideas. This contributed to a focus on Human Freedom and rights. This third seismic shift of Human Freedom pulled society even farther away from the church, and the influence that the church still had began to shrink. Here is a picture of the change:

Christian Freedom

During the Middle Ages, starting at least by the thirteenth century, Europe was further ahead in Human Freedom than any civilization had ever been. By this time the church had decided that slavery was wrong. It implemented this new understanding by extending its sacraments to all slaves, making them Christians, and then imposing a ban on the enslavement of Christians. This effectively abolished slavery in Medieval Europe because, except for small settlements of Jews and the Vikings in the north, *everyone* was at least nominally a Christian (Stark 2013).

Human Freedom

The proclamations against slavery created the first society where all people were free. There were, of course, still many obligations and traditions that demanded much from different groups in the society. In particular, the serfs were bound to the land, but even they were not slaves. Christianity had created the first large, non-slave society. This new freedom, as tentative as it was in some contexts, was the foundation of a new way of thinking. The belief that individuals could and should be free continued to grow through the centuries in these Christian nations.

The start of this movement toward Human Freedom can be identified in the New Testament. We see in the letters of Paul a tacit acceptance of the current institution of slavery, but at the same time, he indicates that, in Christ, all has changed and we are all brothers. He says in Galatians 3:28 that there is not slave or free, but all are one in Christ Jesus. In Philemon he indicates he is sending the slave Onesimus back to his master, but now he needs to be treated like a brother in the Lord.

> no longer as a slave, but better than a slave, as a dear brother. He is very dear to me but even dearer to you, both as a fellow man and as a brother in the Lord. (NIV Philemon 1:16)

In Romans 6:22 he states that we have been set free from sin and have become slaves of God. As a result of these verses, and many others like them, the church began the long process of moving away from the acceptance of slavery and began to promote Human Freedom for everyone.

Freedom for the sake of Freedom

Over time, the freedom to construct our own moral and relational world became the preferred path to human fulfillment. No longer would people settle for trying to find contentment within the relational matrix they were given (Kuehne, 44).

As time went on, common people began to think of "free time" as a concrete expression of personal liberty. It was the time when they got to decide what they wanted to engage in for fun. In increasingly democratic societies, the opportunity to engage in leisure was seen as a right of citizenship (Cross, 76).

Freedom for people to decide what they want to do, based on what they perceive is best for them, is a cherished right in Western society. It has brought amazing good and few of us would want to exchange the freedom we now experience for mindless servitude to the whims of others. Freedom is good, but over time it became separated from its Christian roots to stand alone as a concept. The goal became more and more freedom, for the sake of freedom itself and people conveniently forgot that the source of true freedom was grounded in what God has done for us.

Ultimately, the secular West has sought to maximize individual freedom and will only place limits on it if it is thought to affect another person's individual freedom. As long as one does not criticize other's choices or harm them, then your behavior, no matter what it is, is acceptable (Kuehne, 71).

The Church's Response

When people are permitted to participate in all kinds of activities that harm themselves and others, in the name of being true to oneself, it is clear that society has gone too far with the concept of Human Freedom. People need to be reminded that what really matters is a relationship with other people and God, not just a disembodied freedom concept. Rules can be a positive thing if they enhance the relationships between people, even if they infringe somewhat on the toes of certain individuals' freedoms.

There are certain activities, like sex, that need to stay within the correct boundary of marriage between a man and a women. To those who might protest the limiting of their freedom, the reply would be, that is exactly the point. Maximizing our individual freedom should never have been the main goal.

In the West, we have taken the wonderful Christian principle of freedom and deified it. We, for all intents and purposes, have made a God out of freedom and will attack anyone who does not worship it like we do. The pendulum has swung too far.

Typically, the church has done a poor job in responding. Often it has made the mistake of accepting the scientific world view and then trying to argue against particular activities based on physical harm only. This argument is relatively weak to begin with, but when the physical impediments are overcome, it becomes practically irrelevant.

The solid argument, and the one that has been articulated from the very beginning in Christianity, is that participating in the activity damages the spirit of the one participating in it and harms the spiritual connection between us and others. In the end, if we keep inflicting damage on ourselves, we will cut ourselves off from God and heaven.

Often, the church has come across as bigoted and hypocritical when it talks about sin. I am not questioning the importance of taking a stand for what is right, but it is clear that simply telling people they are going to hell, without explaining the spiritual dimension, is less than helpful.

Another problem the church has had is its penchant for taking strong stands on minor issues. Attempts have been made to limit activities there were not critical to the faith, causing the church to look narrow and behind the times. Choice and fun is something that should have been encouraged, not frowned upon.

In the end, both a poor reaction to critical things and an overreaction to relatively unimportant ones has resulted in a widening gap between church members and typical people in society.

Entertaining the Gospel

As humans became more free, they had greater choice about what activities they engaged in. The natural tendency was to lean toward those activities which were interesting and fun; people wanted to participate in activities or watch events that were entertaining.

People today expect to be entertained and they will not continue to participate in activities which do not interest them.

Unfortunately, many of our churches seem to equate holiness with boredom. Services are not designed to be interesting, and the same activities, in the same order each week, guarantee there are no surprises. If we want to reach the missing generations, we have got to rethink our plan. We can and must present the gospel in ways that are captivating and innovative.

At the same time we must remember that the mediums we use to convey information have an impact on our message. We must always be very careful to identify ways the vehicles of transmission are impacting what we are communicating. The warnings of Neil Postman about amusing ourselves mindlessly are very appropriate to remember. Certainly we do not want to reduce Christianity to only entertainment, stripped of everything that makes it profound and sacred (Postman 1985, 64%). We must avoid making Christianity so much about the fun that the message of Jesus is lost.

Still, nothing must stop us from utilizing every opportunity to spread the gospel. Paul, in his ministry, used every means possible to win others to Christ and we need to do the same. Presenting the gospel in an entertaining way is necessary to reach secular people today and it can be done in a way that stays true to the heart of God.

Chapter 9 - Individual Truth

Summary

The fourth seismic shift between the church and society was Individual Truth. Unlike many other religions, Christianity stresses correct or true doctrine. It was this emphasis on truth that led to the spirit of inquiry and experimentation which characterized the Christian nations during the Middle Ages. Eventually, individualism was taken too far and society made individuals responsible for creating their own worldview from scratch. Relativism said, what is true for you might not be true for me. Personal experience becomes the ultimate authority for making choices. The church tried to take a stand against this type of thinking by holding on to absolutes. This created a gap between church people and people in society, who now see sin more in personal terms.

4th seismic shift: Individual Truth

Very soon after the Human Freedom shift, people began to think in more relative terms about life. One contributor to this was the scientific discoveries of the theory of relativity by Einstein and the uncertainty principle by Heisenberg. This brought about the fourth seismic shift which was Individual Truth. Now the church world began to shrink even more quickly. Here is a picture of the change:

Christian Truth

Christianity is strange because it is an "orthodox" religion which stresses correct (ortho) opinion (doxa), unlike most other religions that are "orthopraxis" and stress correct (ortho) practice (praxis). Because Christianity places a greater emphasis on proper belief, it has consistently concentrated its intellectual energies on the structure of its creeds and theologies (Stark 2007, 6%). This has caused it to favour individual intellectual ability and the search for what is true.

Individual Truth

In addition to the individualist tendency and intellectual direction of the faith as a whole, particular doctrines came to emphasize the individual as well. One of these was the doctrine of free will (Stark 2007, 12%). From the beginning, Christianity emphasized that sin is a personal matter and that it is not primarily a function of the group. Each individual was responsible for his or her own life and actions. For example, when in Acts 5 Ananias and Sapphira lied about the property they sold, they were judged individually, not as a family. This was not typical of most other cultures which stressed the group as a unit was responsible. This focus on the individual was unique and set the Christian faith apart (Stark 2007, 11%).

It is easy to see how, given this theological foundation, a spirit of inquiry and experimentation became prevalent within the Christian nations during the Middle Ages. Once this occurred and society became interested in questioning the truth of everything, some people began to argue against the catholic church dogma. For a time, the church struggled to maintain its unity but eventually it broke apart into different denominations during the Reformation. Still, in each group, individuals did their best to try and figure out what the true or correct theology was.

Eventually, there were individuals who proposed that real truth was found outside the Christian Church, but even this was based on the premise that people needed to find truth for themselves and, at its heart, continues to be the Christian way of thinking. Individuals are responsible for the choices they make, so they need to make good ones and the search for truth is important. These continue to be part of the ethos of Western society up to the present day and this has fueled innovation and discovery on a scale the world has never seen before.

Individualism taken too far

Eventually, society became so focused on the individual that it lost sight of our relationship with others and God. The individual became responsible for constructing their own understanding of the world. Now the quest for truth has become personal. We base our conclusions about what is right based on our own research and personal experiences. Truth is no longer accepted uncritically from parents, government, or church (Dorsett 2012, 9%).

The idea that what might be true for me, might not be true for you, found its way into public thinking via science. In 1927, Werner Heisenberg discovered that it was impossible to measure both the momentum and position of a particle simultaneously. This reintroduction of uncertainty and mystery into human thinking has had a dramatic impact. Society has become quite comfortable with the idea that different people can come to different conclusions, despite the fact that they started with the same evidence. Both of them can be considered to have discovered truth, even if the truths contradict one another. The concept of absolute truth has been replaced with a personal truth for one that will likely vary with the personal truth of another (Dorsett, 9%).

Individual Truth has come to insist that sensory experiences provide the foundation for understanding the world and making choices. Personal experience becomes the ultimate authority in society (Poe 2001, 79). This is very different from basing your life on what some external authority has to say about what you should do.

This individualization of authority has led directly to the rise of philosophical pluralism. The truth now becomes whatever an individual chooses it to be. Tolerance then becomes the chief virtue and if you have conviction that is a vice (Reid, 33%).

Church response to Individual Truth

In modern terms, Individual Truth has come to deny that any philosophy, theology or scientific approach can provide a universal framework for the meaning of human life. People have come to believe that every world view is a human construct that cannot provide any ultimate answers (Kuehne, 59).

The church, when it identified that society was taking the virtue of Individual Truth and turning it into a vice, tried to hold fast to what it considered to be fundamental truth. Denominations differed slightly on exactly what was fundamental, but almost all of them agreed that society had gone too far. In the end, a gap opened up between a society that was becoming more and more relativistic and a church that was trying to maintain core absolutes.

The Individual Truth World

As people stopped blindly accepting what other people told them, they took on the responsibility of constructing their own world view. All metanarratives, including Christianity, became suspect because they were seen as opportunities for people to control others. Normal people became suspicious of any idea that was presented as a completed system, instead of it being built from individual experience.

Trying to connect to people today by starting with the absolutes of the Bible, is a non-starter. These truths are just as powerful as they have always been, but people today will not listen. They think differently. In the past, people went from principles to the particular. Now, the tendency is to go from the particular to the principle.

From the Individual Truth perspective, righteousness is not coming to terms with a Holy God who is concerned about a moral code, but it is about us as people performing right action in the world and getting relationships right with other people. Sin is a life that has not reached its potential and a sense of corporate guilt that we have not made the world the loving place it should be (McNeal 2003, Kindle 43%). These must become our starting points in our conversations that eventually lead to God and what He is like.

Our approach must focus on peoples' own personal idolatry. Coming to a better understanding of their own personal blindness and rebellion will open the road to the theological truth that we have all fallen short of God's glory and missed the mark (Keller, 29%).

Our starting point must be with the personal. People must see themselves or they will not believe us.

Changing our perspective

The church service I was attending was slow. The music was slow, the announcements took forever and the pastor talked at a speed that was practically glacial. All of this was bad, but what was worse was the sermon. It was theologically correct, but unfortunately, it began with general principles that were not supported in any way.

I listened as the pastor talked about characters in the Bible and explained how their lives demonstrated an absolute truth of God. I could see that many people in the church were listening attentively and agreeing with what was being said. It was only as we got to the end of the sermon, that an application of the general truth discussed was connected to our lives. The message was, now that we know the truth, we must apply it.

From a traditional perspective the sermon was excellent, but from an Individual Truth perspective it was a train wreck. I asked my 19-year-old son, after the service was over, if he got anything out of it and he said he got nothing from it at all.

Please note that I am not saying that absolute truth of Christianity is defective in any way. What I am saying is that in order to reach normal people today, we must start from a personal perspective.

Chapter 10 - Digitally Connected

Summary

The fifth seismic shift between the church and society was the Digitally Connected revolution. It was the soil of Christian thinking that paved the way for this shift, because it was oriented to the future instead of trying to worship the past. Today, society has moved from a place of information scarcity, to instant access from almost anywhere. These sweeping changes have created digital issues that never existed before. This has created a gap between church people and people in society who expect to always be Digitally Connected with what is happening.

5th seismic shift: Digitally Connected

As technology continued to develop, it started to do more than transform methods of production or transportation. It began to provide tools that changed how we communicate and think. This latest seismic shift is the ability to be Digitally Connected. Now, the church is something far in the distance that normal people in society do not know very much about at all. Here is a picture of this change:

How Christianity created the Digital World

At first look, it might seem a bit of a stretch to believe that Christianity created the Digital World we live in today but looking a little closer reveals the truth. As we have already seen, it was Christianity that created space for science to flourish and promoted the idea of exploring the world around us in the name of God. It created a Productive Society that provided enough surplus to enable some members of society to focus their energy on solving problems, not just surviving. The gift of Human

Freedom gave people the security to come up with new ideas without fear they would be taken from them by others. Finally, an atmosphere of Individual Truth caused people to find out the truth about how things operated and figure out ways to make improvements.

From its earliest days, Christianity taught that reason was the supreme gift of God and the means to progressively increase our understanding of Him. It was a religion oriented to the future, while many other religions were focused on the past (Stark 2007, 2%). This is why it created the new institution of Universities in the Middle Ages in order to promote learning. It is from this soil that the digital world has sprung.

The Digital Connection Revolution

Before the Internet came along, people operated under the model of scarcity of information. Libraries were built to gather all the precious books together so people would be able to access them. We built schools and staffed them with teachers so the students could come and learn. If you knew something that other people did not, that really mattered. Because information was scarce, it was critical to capture it. Pastors built libraries of books because they never knew when they might need access to a particular piece of information. If they did not keep it close at hand, they might lose it.

This brings us to our first internet era which I have called Capture, although others call it web 0.0. This was a time when the internet existed, but the world wide web did not. The driving force behind the Capture era was to find and then maintain information.

The Capture internet era focused primarily on solving problems that had existed previously, such as capture, storage and retrieval. Tools were created to enable users to search for information that was stored electronically as text or pictures. Programs were developed that allowed people to send text messages to others on the internet (email) and new memory drives were invented to enable the storage of vast quantities of data.

Once people began to get comfortable with using technology in ways that solved existing problems, like storage and retrieval, they began to experiment with new capabilities of the technology to create media-specific content. This Content era, or Web 1.0, saw the rise of technologies that focused on one-way information sharing. Static web pages and blogs pushed content to readers.

The broadcasting of content via the web was similar to other mediums like radio, newspapers and TV, except for the critical difference that the cost of entry into the market was vastly smaller. This encouraged not only many smaller companies to create content, but many individuals began to create it as well. At this point, content became so abundant that figuring out which source to listen to became more and more important.

The next era that internet technology moved into was Conversation. It no longer was enough just to have content being pushed to passive consumers, now people flocked to sites that enabled them to have their own say. This Conversation era, or Web 2.0, saw new technologies that allowed for user feedback and promoted interaction. Wikis allowed anyone to edit them and YouTube made it easy for people to upload video.

The Conversation era promoted read-write websites that took things far beyond what had existed in more traditional mediums. Sites like Amazon, that embraced this change by adding the ability for users to easily comment on products, saw their visitor traffic take off. At this point, we (the people) had become part of the content and dialogue became very important.

The area we now seem to be moving into is Communities (Web 3.0). The Community era has seen the introduction of technologies that promote communities of people. Facebook mimics the relationships you have with real people in the online world and Social Games actually promote sharing and helping out other members of your virtual community.

The Community era promotes technologies that enable virtual interactions with a relatively stable group or clan. Social Games, like Clash of Clans, promote the providing of resources to others and working together to achieve a goal. At this point, we have moved beyond just contributing individually to the conversation, and have actually become part of a virtual group or tribe.

This new paradigm has caused a big issue for many in the church. There has been a switch from tight, local, hierarchical groups, to loose, distributed, networked groups. Some have called this new world, networked individualism (Rainie, 4%). Those who have been accustomed to society operating on the model of tight social groups, are suddenly lost in this new world. This has created a huge gap between many in the church and the rest of society.

Digital Issues

There are those who say that, even as we are doing simple searches, technology has a way of becoming an idol in our hearts (Challies, 10%). It is easy to see why some people take it to the next step and say we would be better off without it. This can be a comforting thought, especially for those who are not comfortable with technology, but it is not a realistic one. The advantages that electronic search and storage bring are too great for most individuals or society to give up. The key is for us to not allow it to become an idol (Challies, 93%).

Some media theorists have pointed out that the medium of the internet has an impact on the messages provided through it; that all of this new content being provided might be suspect, because the true message is getting warped (Detweiler, 11%). It should be acknowledged that every medium has the potential to do this, even the spoken word. The important thing to keep in mind is what potential impact the medium is having on the message and adjust our thinking when necessary.

There are some people who see this less hierarchical internet as an advantage (Drescher, 11%), while others view the fact that technology mediates so many of our interactions with each other, that it is actually making us less human and more alone (Turkle, 8%). It is true that, particularly with the rise of mobile technology and the always-on mentality, there is a loss of opportunities to meditate and contemplate. At the same time, the ability to communicate with more people, more often, is very powerful. Promoting balance in how much time we spend with conversation technology is important.

Others are disturbed that we have lost the tight groups of the past. For them, local hierarchical groups are more comfortable and feel better, but it is good to remember that they also had their own set of issues. Today, for better or worse, we are moving toward a distributed model, where people may participate in a number of networked tribes simultaneously (Rainie, 12%).

Adjusting to the Digital Impact

The impact of technology on modern society means we cannot continue church as usual, if we ever could. Electronic communication is embedded in the everyday life of people and it is not going away. This shift to digital spaces is going to happen whether we want it to or not. Culture has changed and expectations of what churches do must also change. This does not mean the message of the Gospel changes, but the ways in which we present the Good News to society must be in a language they can understand.

We, as the church, must find ways to make the timeless message of Christ meaningful in this new virtual world. The purpose of new virtual communities is not about replacing physical world interaction, but about augmenting it in ways that ensure relationships become stronger. Networked individuals are comfortable with these kinds of structures and are looking for them. The technology connections can reduce the dependence on a physical place to define who is an insider and who is an outsider.

The message of Jesus does not change, but the mediums through which that message is proclaimed must. Current levels of technology usage in our churches are poor to none and this must change if we hope to see them reconnect to society again. Networked individuals are going to demand that we provide content in different ways, and we in the church must respond with appropriate use of technology.

Always On

In the past, activities were segmented and linear. You did one thing at a time and typically activities occurred in the same physical location and at a consistent schedule. The technology that allows us to be Digitally Connected, changes all this. People today expect always to be connected to what is happening.

If what you are doing in your church does not allow a digital access point, then, from the Digitally Connected viewpoint, you are doing it wrong. It is not a matter of some things having a digital component and others not having one; everything you do must take into account the digital world.

Our segmented way of planning and then participating in discrete events, must give way to an always-on mentality. Being Digitally Connected is not an option anymore.

Part 3

How to Cross the Chasm

Now that we have seen just how large the gap is between church people and secular people, it is time to start looking, in more detail, at how this chasm can be crossed for specific elements and programs the church is involved in. Please note that these examples are not guides for things you should implement step by step. They are included here to help you understand the kinds of changes that will make a difference; the kinds of changes that will really connect with people in the real non-church world.

Chapter 11 - Crossing Over

Summary

Even as we seek to cross over and connect with society, we must remember that there are many things we must do correctly for true revival to come. In particular, we must remember that a church of faith must exist or we have no message of hope. Once this has been established, we can use the seismic shifts as stepping stones to help us cross the chasm. The Innovation Gap forces us to have focused vision. Modern Science reminds us to highlight discovery in all we do. Productive Society encourages product excellence. Human Freedom points the way to creating engaging experiences. Individual Truth helps us understand that we must approach things from the personal perspective. Digitally Connected tells us that everything we do must leverage technology properly. All of these things help us to become chasm-crossers who understand how to connect with others around them.

Start with Christianity

As we look at some examples of crossing over in the upcoming chapters, I need to reiterate that these ideas and techniques are of no value if many other critical pieces of church renewal are not dealt with first. Some of these were talked about in chapter 1 and they are foundational to the chasm-crossing model. After all, it matters very little if you get better at explaining the message of your church to people, if the life of God is not present in the congregation. People may come and visit your congregation and say, "What a nice bunch of people," but have little impetus to return. How different the picture will be if they experience the power of God while they are with you. Without a gathered community being transformed by God, there is no point in even trying to cross the chasm.

First identify why we need to cross

I was running late and was pushing the speed of the car as fast as I dared. I had preached at this church before, but had forgotten exactly how far away it was. Arriving breathless and only a couple minutes late, I got the service started. When I got to the sermon, I made a comment about remembering on the way there that the car clock was wrong and that I had asked Siri (a voice activated digital assistant on the iPhone) what time it was. Receiving a wall of blank stares in response to my statement. I quickly switched to explaining that I had checked my phone.

I know there are churches where many people would have immediately understood what I meant when I said Siri, but it was experiences like this that showed me how large the gap between many church people and regular people in society had really become.

If the message of Jesus is going to be proclaimed to people in our society in a way they can understand it then the chasm has to be crossed. Since people in society will not cross over to us it is critical that church members learn how to cross over to them.

Using seismic shifts as stepping stones

I am now going to talk about one way we can think about crossing the chasm. I am not by any means recommending this as the only or even the best way, but it will help explain how a program can be made to jump the chasm. To do this, we will be using, as stepping stones, the very things that created the gap. For those who have played electronic platformer games, you can think of each seismic shift being transformed into platforms. You must jump from one to the other in order to make it all the way across the chasm in one piece.

A Chasm Crossing Church

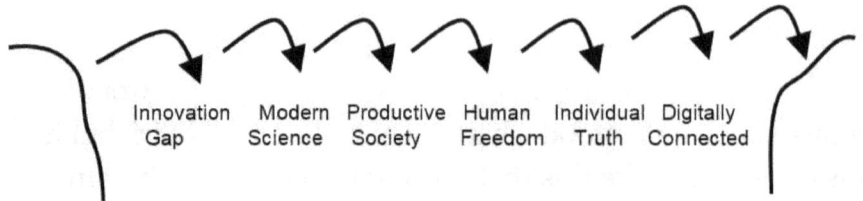

The Innovation Gap has always been a part of the challenge to the innovative Christian message and is not a new seismic shift, but I have included it because it still contributes to the chasm we must cross.

The purpose in making sure we include elements in our programs that address each of these areas is not to water down the truth, but to ensure our message can be heard in a culture that is used to experiencing things in a different way. We certainly must be careful not to rely too heavily on any of these ideas and risk losing the gospel message, but this must be balanced with us speaking in a language that the surrounding culture can understand. To do this, each of these ideas must be addressed.

Positive aspects of the shifts

It is also important to remember that, although we can view each of the seismic shifts in very negative ways (and they do have their problems), we can also find elements in each of these that are very good. It is these good things that we want to utilize to propel the Gospel forward.

Here is a summary of the major positive contribution that each shift brings and how regular people will expect to see this implemented in whatever program we do.

Innovation Gap	You must be a small market leader; they must be able to trust you.
Modern Science	Discovery must be highlighted; they must feel it is an adventure.
Productive Society	Experience must be customized; they must have a say.
Human Freedom	There must be an element of fun; they must not be bored.
Individual Truth	Starting point is relative experiences; they must see themselves.
Digitally Connected	Technology must be part of any solution; they must be able to be digital.

Innovation Gap requires us to have Focused Vision

The Innovation Gap is a reminder that any created program should be focused on a small market segment. If you do not become the market leader, then you will not be able to generate any momentum for your program. In the past, churches tried to offer many different programs in an effort to meet as many needs as possible. Typically, this meant doing a number of things poorly. Keeping things focused helps eliminate this problem. We must not be fooled into thinking that marketing principles are all we need, but we must allow the advantages of focus to help us create programs that succeed phenomenally and translate into people having the feeling that they can trust us.

The key idea for the Innovation Gap is Focused Vision. All of our activities and programs must be driven by the vision, always asking the question, does the thing we are trying to do fit with what the church believes it is called to do? Most importantly, is it a small enough vision? Does it focus on a particular area and aim to make a big difference in a small market?

Modern Science requires us to Highlight Discovery

Modern Science shows us that our programs must highlight discovery. Science is always about discovering new truths and people have come to expect this. This is easy to do if we get intentional about it, since the gospel has always been about new good news. Participants must see that they are progressing toward some goal and discovering the truth of God. Results matter to people who live in our modern scientific culture and they must be incorporated into what we do. We must not permit our fascination with results and new understanding to take over, but allow the positive contributions of science and modern techniques to point the way to an improved relationship with God and others.

The key idea for Modern Science is to Highlight Discovery. The entire activity of science is wrapped up in the process of experimenting to find new knowledge and publishing the results. All of our activities and programs must aim to discover more of what God is calling each one of us to be and do. The idea that "this is the way we have always done it" cannot become our standard. Our goal must be to discover what God wants us to do as a church.

Productive Society requires us to have Product Excellence

Productive Society shows that the programs we create must be more flexible and maintain a higher level of quality customer service. We must not fall into the trap of catering to every whim, but utilize the advantages of productivity to create higher quality programs and more interactive experiences for all who participate.

The key idea for Productive Society is Product Excellence. Because we want everyone to experience the love of God, all of our activities and programs must aim to reach a high standard of excellence. Good enough is no longer good enough. Our goal is to achieve the highest quality possible, given the resources that are available. Just knowing this fact will encourage church members to care more about the final product. This will work well if we have already reduced the number of things we are trying to achieve, so we can ensure that the projects we do are completed to a higher level of excellence.

Human Freedom requires us to have Engaging Experience

Human Freedom points out that within the programs we create, there must reside an element of fun. Participants expect to be entertained and have fun. It is not true, as some seem to believe, that suffering through a long and boring service makes you more holy. In reality, it just makes you more sleepy. In today's media-saturated society, boring is a sin and people will not listen to your message unless you grab their attention. We must not cheapen the message of grace, but allow the advantages of freedom to create a captivating and appealing gospel message.

The key idea for Human Freedom is Engaging Experience. All of our activities and programs must be designed to be interesting. Boring is a word that we never want to hear. Our goal is to create engaging experiences for everyone who is involved with us. Entertainment is not a dirty word and we should be using all possible methods to spread the love of God, including making people laugh and enjoy themselves. There will always be a place for the tough subjects and difficult conversations, but even these can be covered in an interesting way. Creating Engaging Experiences should be what our churches do.

Individual Truth requires us to have Personal Perspective

Individual Truth shows us that the starting point for any program must be personal. People will not listen for very long if we start our arguments off in the absolute realm. The days of arguing deductively, from general statements of faith, are gone. They expect our starting point to be relative experiences which then can build inductively toward big truths. We must be careful not to lose absolutes, but allow the advantages of Individual

Truth to help us create programs in which people can see themselves.

The key idea for Individual Truth is Personal Perspective. All of our activities and programs must start by talking about personal experiences. Just as Paul shared his story of faith before Agrippa, so we too must declare what we have experienced to others. The sharing of personal stories must never be used as additional illustrations, but should be the actual foundation on which our arguments are built. Our goal is to show people themselves and what their hearts are really like. Coming at things from a personal perspective will enable us to connect to regular people in society and show them the way to deeper truths of the faith.

Digitally Connected requires us to Leverage Technology

Digitally Connected reminds us that all of our programs must contain a technology component. This is not included as an afterthought, but needs to be included from the very beginning as an integral part of what we do. People today live in a digital world and asking them to leave it when they enter the church doors is like asking a fish to leave the water. It is survivable for short periods, but the long term prognosis is not good. We must not become enraptured by the technology, but allow the advantages of being Digitally Connected to create programs that enable people to be digital.

The key idea for Digitally Connected is to Leverage Technology. All of our activities and programs must include a technology component. In some cases, modern digital technology may completely replace the way we did things in the past. In other cases, it will just be a part of the solution, but in all cases it must be present. Our goal is to make programs that normal people feel comfortable relating to.

Key idea from each Chasm component

Here are the chasm components and the corresponding main idea we need to keep in mind as we evaluate programs and activities in our churches.

Chasm	Main Idea
Innovation Gap	Focused Vision
Modern Science	Highlight Discovery
Productive Society	Product Excellence
Human Freedom	Engaging Experience
Individual Truth	Personal Perspective
Digitally Connected	Leverage Technology

The First step we will take to cross the chasm is to evaluate programs based on Focused Vision. Then we will consider

Highlght Discovery, followed by Product Excellence. After this we will do Engaging Experience. Then we will do Personal Perspective and finish with Leverage Technology.

Step 1	Step 2	Step 3	Step 4	Step 5	Step 6
Focused Vision	Highlight Discovery	Product Excellence	Engaging Experience	Personal Perspective	Leverage Technology

Becoming a Chasm Crosser

If your church is sufficiently healthy, you may want to start looking at how some of your programs could be modified in order to take them across the chasm. To start this, I would recommend that any activities your church undertakes be evaluated according to the chasm criteria and given a chasm score. Evaluating your programs will bring understanding on where your church currently stands and help you plan for the future. You can then identify one small area where you will implement some tiny changes to bring up the chasm score of that particular program. Only make changes in one area at a time and evaluate each change before making any more. If you make more than one change at the same time, it can be difficult to know which thing you have done is actually making the difference.

Preface every change with the words, "We are going to try this for ____ (amount of time) and then evaluate it." If we learn the change has had a positive effect, we can consider implementing it, as a church. If it does not work for this particular congregation, we have learned what not to do. Either way, you are preparing your congregation for success instead of leaving the door open to failure. This will also significantly reduce the antagonism and opposition you might receive from members who do not like the change.

The last few chapters will give you hypothetical examples of how particular tasks and programs can be evaluated based on the seismic shifts, and then possible ways they can be modified to help a particular congregation cross the chasm. These examples are NOT included because I think they are the most critical areas I think we need to change, but simply to provide concrete examples of what might be possible.

Chapter 12 - Church Offering

Summary

Our motivation to improve our church's offering must come from a deep desire for others to know the truth about God, not from a desire to increase our bank accounts. Currently, the way many churches receive donations connects poorly to the seismic shifts. We can greatly improve how we handle the offering in our churches.

What is our offering motivation?

As we look at offering in this chapter, it is important to keep in mind that real change in the church must always be built on a spiritual foundation. As much as it may be helpful to understand ways to make how we accept donations more efficient and connect better with people in our society, it will mean nothing if our heart motivation is wrong.

If the goal is to raise more money in order to keep programs running and the doors open, we have a serious problem. It may well be that we have replaced our faith in God, with faith in money. Until this issue is resolved, the church will not be open to be transformed by the power of God.

Our motivation for improving the offering experience must be about us wanting others to have the opportunity to experience the transforming love and grace of God, like we have. We give, that others may come to faith in God. If we are not experiencing this change in our own hearts, then this must be our first priority. We must allow the truth of God's love to seep into our souls and only then will changes in how we do offering make sense.

Evaluating church offering based on the seismic shifts

Now we are going to evaluate offering as it is currently being done in many churches, against the six factors that need to be addressed in order to cross the chasm: Focused Vision, Highlight Discovery, Product Excellence, Engaging Experience, Personal Perspective, and Leverage Technology. We will use a 1 -

5 scale to evaluate each of them where 1 is poor and 5 is excellent.

Collecting offering is an important task, but it is not one that is very labor intensive, nor does it require a lot of planning. Because it is relatively simple, it will help us see more clearly how the Crossing the Chasm model works.

Focused Vision for Church Offering

Most churches explain that the offering they are collecting is for the church to meet expenses in order to continue to proclaim the gospel in the local community. They may also indicate how some of the offering will be used to help people who are experiencing financial hardship.

Many churches do a good job of tying giving to worship and faith. Members are encouraged to see contributing to God's work as an act of faith; to approach giving as another way they worship God.

Although there are some churches that have slipped into approaching offering as fund-raising, most approach it with proper reverence and clearly explain the big picture of what is going on. What they often fail to do is connect offering with the specific vision of the church.

This failure to connect church offering with the vision to which God has called that particular church, means we would have to give most churches only a 3 for Focused Vision in regard to church offering.

What is needed are churches that have identified a particular vision, no matter what that is, and can then connect this with why the church is taking up offering. It might be that the church has a vision for the homeless in the community. It could be it has a vision for single mothers. Perhaps it has a vision to be the place unchurched people will want to attend or a church that gives people a break from the technology that surrounds them.

No matter what the vision is, what is important is that the vision is small enough to give the congregation focus and then the offering becomes an opportunity to highlight, once again, the purpose and calling of this particular congregation.

Churches that manage to do this may be able to increase their Focused Vision level to 5 for church offering.

Highlight Discovery for Church Offering

Most churches do a good job during the announcements section of the service, highlighting things the church is involved in for members and the surrounding community. Where they are a bit weaker, is linking these activities more strongly with the offering that is typically taken up later in the service.

There is a real danger that people may come to perceive offering as what we need to give in order to keep programs and services going, instead of linking it more directly with the new work God is doing in the community.

Many churches would wind up with a score of 3 for Highlighting Discovery with regard to church offering.

What is needed are churches that are intentional in connecting their vision to the offering and will look for opportunities to highlight what has been done to meet their missional goals. If the vision is to reach homeless people, then a short video about a new project to provide shelter, or an interview with a person who has been helped, would be shown.

Providing church members with the opportunity to discover what has been happening with regard to the mission of the church will make a huge difference to people. The scientific mind wants to see how effective we are being in ministry.

Churches that are able to do this may be able to increase their Highlight Discovery level to 5 for Church Offering.

Product Excellence for Church Offering

Churches typically do the very best they can to steward the money that comes in. Budgets help clarify how the money is to be spent and this is important and necessary. Often though, a problem that can occur where the focus becomes meeting the budget instead of funding ministry.

Churches try and maintain as many programs as they can, with ever shrinking funds. By focusing more on what we are trying to support rather than the core mission of the local church, we get off track.

Many churches would wind up with a score of 2 for Product Excellence with regard to Church Offering.

What is needed are churches that focus on their vision so they will have the advantage of knowing in which areas to increase funding and which areas to reduce. They will also tend to benefit from increased giving because members will clearly know what their donations are going to support.

It is important in our current culture to let people know exactly what they are supporting and it would likely be beneficial to even provide information from time to time that indicates how much money is going to support the primary mission of the church.

Churches that are able to do this may be able to increase their Product Excellence level to 4 for Church Offering.

Engaging Experience for Church Offering

Many churches are very clear that offering should be a worshipful experience. They provide an atmosphere, prayer and music that help those attending to worship God as they give.

There are some churches, however, that have gotten so desperate for funds that they crowd out the message of "we worship God with our giving" with "we need your money now or the doors close." There are others that have cheapened the experience by no longer making offering a separate event and simply send buckets around while the congregation is singing. Both of these approaches are less than ideal.

Many churches would wind up with a score of 4 for Engaging Experience with regard to Church Offering.

What is needed are churches that do all they can to make the unique experience of worshiping God through giving more engaging and personal. Occasionally changing the format of how they run the offering time would help keep the event fresh in the minds of the people.

It must be our goal to make the process of worshiping God through giving interesting; giving people an opportunity to have a real encounter with God, who is most certainly not boring.

Churches that are able to do this may be able to increase their Engaging Experience level to 5 for Church Offering.

Personal Perspective for Church Offering

Many churches indicate to attendees that we give because God has given to us and that everything we have comes from Him. While this is theologically correct, it does not connect well to the current culture.

The message that many of our guests may get, who attend our church on a Sunday morning, is that we want their money. They see our request for money in relative terms, not buying into the more absolute concept of giving God what belongs to Him.

Many churches would wind up with a score of 3 for Personal Perspective with regard to Church Offering.

What is needed are churches who tell guests that they should let the plate pass by without feeling any pressure to contribute, explaining that members contribute because it is an act of worship by them to God.

This will reduce the anxiety that some guests may feel and may even increase their curiosity about what being a member is all about. For church members this will once again solidify why they are giving.

Churches that are able to do this may be able to increase their Personal Perspective level to 4 for Church Offering.

Leverage Technology for Church Offering

Many churches still only provide offering plates where members can give cash or checks. The problem with this is that more and more people are not even carrying cash with them. It is important to provide a digital way that people can contribute to the church and its ministries.

Many churches would wind up with a score of 1 for Leverage Technology with regard to Church Offering.

What is needed are churches moving in the direction of digital transactions and encouraging pre-authorized giving. People choose the level they want to give each month and it is automatically transferred from their bank account. Moving giving to the digital sphere will connect well with what the average person in society would expect.

Churches that are able to do this may be able increase their Leverage Technology level to 5 for Church Offering.

Summary of Results for Church Offering

Chasm Factor	Current Offering	New Offering
Focused Vision	3	5
Highlight Discovery	3	5
Product Excellence	2	4
Engaging Experience	4	5
Personal Perspective	3	4
Leverage Technology	1	5
Totals	16/30	28/30
Percent	53%	93%

Most churches will not be able to increase the effectiveness of the offering by this large amount, but that is not the point. What this gap between current practice and potential future practice identifies is that there is great opportunity for improvement in the area of offering.

I believe that if churches evaluated how they are currently doing offering in light of the chasm factors, many would identify this as an area in which they can make improvements. It is certainly something that will help them connect better to the younger generations.

Keep things in perspective

One of the main reasons I have included specific examples in the final chapters is because I want to help people understand the kinds of things they need to be thinking about as they look to make changes in churches. I believe, sometimes, churches make the mistake of thinking that just a few minor changes will be all that it will take but for real change to occur. The fact is, we need to get a lot of things right.

At the same time, I do not want those who are more digitally challenged to simply give up because they believe they will never understand technology. I would state that it is possible for them to do more than they think and would also say that it is not all up to them. There are people in many congregations who are digitally competent enough to lead the way. We do not have to do this all by ourselves, but must move forward as a team.

Chapter 13 - Congregation Communication

Summary

When we think about trying to improve the communication of important information to members of the congregation, we must be careful to not let our focus get too distracted from the vertical communication we need to have with God. Currently, the way many churches communicate, via paper bulletins and other media, does an OK job connecting to the seismic shifts, but changing how communication takes place could be an opportunity to make a bigger impact.

Keep your relationship with God vibrant

As we consider communication in this chapter, we must not fall into the trap of emphasizing horizontal relationships with others over the vertical relationship we have with God. In churches, we often have a tendency to focus on communicating with each other and neglect communicating with God.

Renewal in churches will only take place when we allow our relationship with God to impact our relationship with others. As we read scripture and pray, we need to ask God to speak to us. We need to listen to what the Holy Spirit is trying to say to us and the church. We must let God speak to our hearts that we are truly loved, and believe, by faith, that He will guide us by the Holy Spirit.

Changing our bulletins or websites, without changing our communication patterns with God, will do little for us; but if we do get serious about our relationship with God, then altering how we connect with others can make sense.

Evaluating Congregation Communication based on the seismic shifts

Next we will examine Congregation Communication as it is currently being done in many churches, against the six factors that need to be addressed in order to cross the chasm: Focused Vision, Highlight Discovery, Product Excellence, Engaging

Experience, Personal Perspective, and Leverage Technology. We will again use a 1 - 5 scale to evaluate each of them where 1 is poor and 5 is excellent.

Creating bulletins, updating web pages and using social media to provide information to people about the church and upcoming events, is very valuable, but it takes more effort to create them than most people would suspect. Again, we will evaluate the results of these mediums using the chasm model.

Focused Vision for Congregation Communication

Many churches provide only a paper bulletin, which does a reasonable job of providing information if you attend on Sunday. If they have a website it may not be updated regularly and the same can be said for social media channels.

The biggest issue they have, though, is the communication channels they do use are not focused on the vision for the congregation. Typically, a hodge podge of information about the church and the surrounding community is presented. Normally it would be difficult to identify what the church is all about.

Many churches would wind up with a score of 1 for Focused Vision with regard to Congregation Communication.

What is needed are churches that begin to use different media to connect to people in the modern world. Each one should be utilized to remind members and potential members what the church's ultimate vision is. Before they press send, each creator of information should ask the questions: "Does this communication put us closer to or further away from the vision?" and "Have I included something that will remind people about what our vision is together?"

Remember it is Focused Vision that is our first stepping stone across the Chasm.

```
Step 1
Focused
Vision
```

A specific vision is critical because we are trying to bring the gospel to a non-Christian culture.

Churches that are able to do this may be able to increase their Focused Vision level to 5 for Congregation Communications.

Highlight Discovery for Congregation Communication

Many churches use media (bulletins, web pages, Facebook, Twitter) to send information to members of the congregation. Most do a relatively good job of broadcasting information through these media.

What is often missing is feedback to ensure that real two-way communication takes place. In today's culture it is not enough to only tell people things. Churches must become good listeners too.

Many churches would wind up with a score of 3 for Highlight Discovery with regard to Congregation Communication.

What is needed are churches that know communication must be a two-way flow and will build opportunities to make sure this takes place. They will keep testing to see if the message is getting through. This can vary from a quick show of hands during a service, to online surveys.

Remember it is Highlight Discovery that is our second stepping stone across the Chasm.

Discovery is critical because we are trying to bring the gospel to a scientific culture.

Churches that are able to do this may be able to increase their Highlight Discovery level to 5 for Congregation Communication.

Product Excellence for Congregation Communication

Often churches spend significant time making sure that their paper bulletins are a quality product. Unfortunately less time is spent ensuring that websites and Facebook pages reach the same quality standards.

Many churches would wind up with a score of 3 for Product Excellence with regard to Congregation Communication.

What is needed are churches that recognize it is more important in today's culture to have the digital face of the church (website, Facebook) at even a higher level of excellence than the bulletin.

Remember, it is Product Excellence that is our third stepping stone across the Chasm.

Step 3
Product Excellence

Excellence is critical because we are trying to bring the gospel to a productive culture.

Churches that are able to do this may be able to increase their Product Excellence level to 4 for Congregation Communication.

Engaging Experience for Congregation Communication

Often churches go to quite a bit of effort to make their bulletins interesting. However, a once a week interaction is not enough in today's western culture.

Many churches would wind up with a score of 3 for Engaging Experience with regard to Congregation Communication.

What is needed are churches that make sure there is a more constant flow of information about things that their members might find interesting. We need to keep the lines of communication open, and updating a Twitter account is an excellent start in this direction.

Remember, it is Engaging Experience that is our fourth stepping stone across the Chasm.

Step 4
Engaging Experience

Engagement is critical because we are trying to bring the gospel to a culture that values freedom.

Churches that are able to do this may be able to increase their Engaging Experience level to 5 for Congregation Communication.

Personal Perspective for Congregation Communication

Many churches are good at creating face to face community. In fact, for some, F2F may be the only form of community that exists. Given that virtual communication is becoming more and more common, this is a situation that needs to change.

I have seen some churches use Facebook as yet another broadcast medium, but this is ignoring the major strength of this platform. Facebook was made to create connections between people.

Many churches would wind up with a score of 3 for Personal Perspective with regard to congregation communication.

What is needed is for churches to understand that they must use tools like Facebook to create virtual communities.

Remember, it is Personal Perspective that is our fifth stepping stone across the Chasm.

```
        Step 5
    ┌─────────────┐
    │  Personal   │
    │ Perspective │
    └─────────────┘
```

A personal starting point is critical, because we are trying to bring the gospel to a culture that values personal truth.

Churches that are able to do this may be able to increase their Personal Perspective level to 4 for Congregation Communication.

Leverage Technology for Congregation Communication

Often churches acknowledge that they need to use digital tools to communicate, and this is a good thing. The challenge is to begin to use them effectively.

Many churches would wind up with a score of 2 for Leverage Technology with regard to Congregation Communication.

Congregation Communication

What is needed are churches that will start to make digital communication their top priority.

Remember, it is technology that is our sixth stepping stone across the Chasm.

```
Step 6
┌──────────┐
│ Leverage │
│Technology│
└──────────┘
```

Leveraging Technology is critical because we are trying to bring the gospel to a digital culture.

Churches that are able to do this may be able to increase their Leverage Technology level to 5 for congregation communication.

Summary of Results for Congregation Communication

Chasm Factor	Current Methods	New Methods
Focused Vision	1	5
Highlight Discovery	3	5
Product Excellence	3	4
Engaging Experience	3	5
Personal Perspective	3	4
Leverage Technology	2	5
Totals	15/30	28/30
Percent	50%	93%

    It is important to keep in mind that we are using Chasm factors to help us identify areas where we can improve Congregation Communication and the reason I provide specific numbers is to help clarify how significant this change could be. Certainly where individual churches start in the process and what they will be able to accomplish in their particular context will vary greatly.

I do expect though that addressing the issue of Congregation Communications would help many churches connect better with regular people in society. The only caveat is that this change is relatively challenging from a technological standpoint, so it might not be the best place to start with a technology-challenged congregation.

The bigger picture

Part of figuring out where we want to go, requires us to know where we do not want to go. We need to get comfortable with evaluating particular options and finding out they will not work, or at least will not work at this particular time. Learning what not to do is just as important as learning what we should do.

We need to not become overwhelmed by the journey that is placed before us. We must not shrink back in fear. We must not say, "I could never do this." What is required of us is to begin small steps of change that will lead us to solutions that will work.

Chapter 14 - Preaching Presentation

Summary

As we look at trying to make our preaching more effective, it is important to remember that our message needs to always remain one of grace, not guilt and works. Currently, the way most churches experience preaching does not speak to typical people in society. We need to change how we preach, so we are speaking in a way that better connects to the seismic shifts.

Preaching God's message

It is possible to improve the communication level of preaching, but lose the message. People may come to like and connect better with what we are saying, but we may no longer be true to the gospel.

Many churches and leaders need to fully accept the Good News: God has done for us in Christ what we could not do for ourselves. We must be very careful not to slip into trying to achieve our standing before God, based on the good works we do. When our focus slips to our efforts, we have, in essence, rejected the good gift of grace God has given us.

Preaching that is based on guilt and trying to cajole the members to work harder and do more, will never achieve success in the long run. All that we do must be based on what God has done in us. We are not working to make ourselves holy, but allowing the Holiness of God to permeate our beings. This must be the basis for our preaching and then any changes we make to improve it will be valuable.

Evaluating current preaching based on the seismic shifts

Now let us evaluate preaching as it is currently being done in many churches, against the six factors that need to be addressed in order to cross the chasm: Focused Vision, Highlight Discovery, Product Excellence, Engaging Experience, Personal Perspective, and Leverage Technology. We will again use a 1 - 5 scale to evaluate each of them, where 1 is poor and 5 is excellent.

Focused Vision for Preaching Presentation

Typically, in churches, pastors cover a wide variety of theological topics in their sermons. This is valuable because the people need to understand the basis for their Christian faith. At the same time, there can be a failure to clearly connect the many messages with the vision that the local congregation has been called to fulfill.

Many churches would wind up with a score of 3 for Focused Vision with regard to Preaching Presentation.

What is needed are churches that make it a point to ensure every sermon draws attention to the church mission, and once or twice a year devote the entire sermon to this important topic.

The Innovation Gap (between Christian and non-Christian cultures) requires us to use Focused Vision so we can connect with people in western society.

Churches that are able to do this may be able to increase their Focused Vision level to 4 for Preaching Presentation.

Highlight Discovery for Preaching Presentation

In most churches, sermons typically follow a very logical process, which is great. Where they get into trouble is that there is no way to evaluate whether or not the congregation has discovered anything new. There is no indicator that progress is being made.

Many churches would wind up with a score of 3 for Highlight Discovery with regard to Preaching Presentation.

What is needed are churches that provide the pastor with feedback regarding how the people are processing the material. This could take the form of a small group that gets together with the pastor to share their experiences. Another possibility is actually incorporating some form of testing while the sermon is ongoing.

Modern Science requires us to use methods that Highlight Discovery so we can connect with people in western society.

Churches that are able to do this would may be able to increase their Highlight Discovery level to 5 for Preaching Presentation.

Product Excellence for Preaching Presentation

Many churches have pastors that work very hard to create sermons that will enlighten the church members and teach them about the Christian faith. They normally do the best they can, but typically these sermons are created in isolation with little input from church members. This almost guarantees that the sermon will not be as effective as it would have been if the congregation had been able to provide input.

Many churches would wind up with a score of 3 for Product Excellence with regard to Preaching Presentation.

What is needed are churches that encourage interactions between the people and the pastor as the sermon is being created. For example, a week before the message will be presented, the pastor could start creating the sermon on a wiki that others can view if they want to and provide feedback. Later on, the pastor might send out, via electronic media (email and Facebook), a link to a video that congregants can take a look at before Sunday, and any comments received can be incorporated into the sermon's construction.

Productive Society requires us to make sure our programs maintain a high level of Product Excellence so they will connect with people in western society.

Churches that are able to do this would may be able to increase their Product Excellence level to 4 for Preaching Presentation.

Engaging Experience for Preaching Presentation

Most churches do the best they can to make people feel welcome. The problem is that most sermons are not often fun or memorable.

Many churches would wind up with a score of 2 for Engaging Experience with regard to Preaching Presentation.

What is needed are churches that encourage the pastor to use a number of different media (images, video, and audio) to demonstrate what they are talking about. They might even include opportunities for clicker apps that people can use on their smartphones in order to ask questions while the sermon is ongoing. The question is asked and a response could then be shared with everyone.

Human Freedom requires us to make sure our programs provide an Engaging Experience so they will connect with people in western society.

Churches that are able to do this may be able to increase their Engaging Experience level to 4 for Preaching Presentation.

Personal Perspective for Preaching Presentation

Most churches have pastors who do their best to take the principles from the Bible and help people see how these can be applied to their lives, and this is important. An area of weakness however, is that they don't approach the material from a personal level.

Many churches would wind up with a score of 2 for Personal Perspective with regard to Preaching Presentation.

What is needed are churches that encourage their pastors to approach theological concepts starting from the individual level. By including stories of people in the congregation (with their permission of course), you create something that people can relate to.

Personal Truth requires us to make sure our programs start from a Personal Perspective so they will connect with people in western society.

Churches that are able to do this may be able to increase their Personal Perspective level to 5 for Preaching Presentation.

Leverage Technology for Preaching Presentation

Many churches that utilize technology well display information during the service like announcements and song lyrics. A weaker area is providing information while the sermon is ongoing.

Many churches would wind up with a score of 3 for Leverage Technology with regard to Preaching Presentation.

What is needed are churches that utilize technology to take the sermon beyond just a verbal presentation. They must utilize multimedia to effectively get the message across.

Digitally Connected requires us to make sure our programs Leverage Technology so they will connect with people in western society.

Churches that are able to do this may be able to increase their Leverage Technology level to 5 for Preaching Presentation.

Summary of Results for Preaching Presentation

Chasm Factor	Current Preaching	New Preaching
Focused Vision	3	4
Highlight Discovery	3	5
Product Excellence	3	4
Engaging Experience	2	4
Personal Perspective	2	5
Leverage Technology	3	5
Totals	16/30	27/30
Percent	53%	90%

Some people may disagree with the numbers I have selected for Current Preaching and argue they are too low. In your particular context that may be true, but the big take away is how can we improve preaching by paying attention to Chasm factors. What can we do differently to reach more people in society through preaching?

Churches need to pay careful attention to this area because improvements to Preaching Presentation, will pay big dividends. Numerous studies I have read have indicated that powerful preaching was one of the most important factors that caused people to begin attending a church.

The real goal

The real goal of the examples I am sharing in these final chapters is not that you would run out and implement them immediately. Likewise, they are not here to discourage you or make the task feel impossible. They exist to help you understand that there are things which can be done to bring about real change in churches, even though, for many people, this may be difficult to comprehend. I want you to see that the solution to stopping the decline in churches is more difficult than we thought, but at the same time, there is hope.

Chapter 15 - Chasm Crossers

Summary

In this final chapter, we will be looking at how churches can help train members to become Chasm Crossers. In doing this, it is critical that the people have fully allowed God's vision to become their own. Currently, the way churches train people to connect missionally with society is very poor. Updating our training to better connect with the shifts is critical.

The Heart of Local Missions

The purpose of doing local missions is not so church members can feel better about themselves, but that reaching out to others is central to who God is. He is a God of Love who desires us to also love people with His love. If our goal is to be more effective in reaching others so that the number of people attending church increases, we have the wrong perspective.

It is possible to start viewing people based on what they can do for us and the church. The problem is that simply increasing the number of attendees on Sunday is not what God wants, if the people are not coming into a vibrant relationship with Him.

We must allow God's vision to become our vision. He crossed over to us that we might cross over to others. Our desire to help others must be based on love and sacrifice, not on control. If we allow God's love to flow out of us, then improving training for local missions will be valuable.

Evaluating Chasm Crossing preparation based on the seismic shifts

Now let us evaluate the preparation of Chasm Crossers as it is currently being done in many churches, against the six factors that need to be addressed in order to cross the chasm: Focused Vision, Highlight Discovery, Product Excellence, Engaging Experience, Personal Perspective and Leverage Technology. We will again use a 1 - 5 scale to evaluate each of them where 1 is poor and 5 is excellent.

Focused Vision for Chasm Crossers

Most churches do a good job presenting the Christian faith, but they struggle with teaching members how to be missional in our current culture. Often they do not have any particular group or program that is tasked with addressing this issue. In many cases, there is a complete lack of understanding of what the changes are, let alone how they should be addressed.

Many churches would wind up with a score of 1 for Focused Vision with regard to Chasm Crossers.

What is needed are churches that use the vision of the church to make Chasm Crossing a priority. They would address the issues that church people are going to have when they talk to typical people in society. They would understand that we must change how we speak to people about the gospel and factor in that it is as if we are talking to someone from a different culture.

Keep in mind that we must have Focused Vision, because we no longer live in a Christian culture.

Churches that are able to do this may be able to increase their Focused Vision level to 5 for Chasm Crossers.

Highlight Discovery for Chasm Crossers

Many churches occasionally use the Sunday sermon to address some of the changes in society and this is a good thing. Unfortunately, this is often not done methodically and there is typically no follow-up.

Many churches would wind up with a score of 2 for Highlight Discovery with regard to Chasm Crossers.

What is needed are churches that have realized that, in addition to ensuring that preaching addresses the seismic shifts in their own right, there needs to be an emphasis on how Christians must engage the new cultural reality. Examples of what to do and what not to do would be very helpful. Small groups might facilitate the flow of information to people about this important area.

Keep in mind that we must Highlight Discovery because we no longer live in a pre-scientific culture.

Churches that are able to do this would likely increase their Highlight Discovery level to 4 for Chasm Crossers.

Product Excellence for Chasm Crossers

Many churches desire to reach out effectively to the people in their communities. Unfortunately, little time is actually spent preparing church members on how to understand and interact with normal society, and any training that does occur is often done poorly.

Many churches would wind up with a score of 1 for Product Excellence with regard to Chasm Crossers.

What is needed are churches that create courses about the basic shifts in society, delivering them both in face to face groups and using virtual spaces.

Keep in mind that we must have Product Excellence, because we no longer live in a pre-industrial culture.

Churches that are able to do this may be able to increase their Product Excellence level to 3 for Chasm Crossers.

Engaging Experience for Chasm Crossers

Often churches are prepared to answer spiritual questions of members and attenders and this is very good. Typically though, there is no opportunity for people to bring the questions they have about being missionaries to the current culture.

Many churches would wind up with a score of 1 for Engaging Experience with regard to Chasm Crossers.

What is needed are churches that create on-going groups that allow people who are trying to cross the chasm to talk with others who are attempting to do the same thing. Helping people understand that they are not crazy and that the changes have been huge, would be very helpful.

Keep in mind that we must have Engaging Experiences, because we no longer live in a fixed-role culture.

Churches that are able to do this may be able to increase their Engaging Experience level to 5 for Chasm Crossers.

Personal Perspective for Chasm Crossers

Many churches provide opportunities for members to share their personal, spiritual journeys. This may be through a lay witness time, in adult Sunday school or small group, and this is great. The opportunities for people to share how they have witnessed to others is not encouraged as much.

Many churches would wind up with a score of 3 for Personal Perspective with regard to Chasm Crossers.

What is needed are churches that recognize the importance of having people share their experiences of witnessing with the entire church, highlighting how church thinking needs to change in order to connect with those who may have never attended church.

Keep in mind that we are must start with Personal Perspective because we no longer live in an absolute truth culture.

Churches that are able to do this may be able to increase their Personal Perspective level to 4 for Chasm Crossers.

Leverage Technology for Chasm Crossers

Many churches utilize technology in the church service by operating an audio system and a presentation system during the service and this is wonderful. Unfortunately, many are not using technology to address the Chasm issue.

Many churches would wind up with a score of 1 for Leverage Technology with regard to Chasm Crossers.

What is needed are churches that create courses, with an online course system, to address this issue. It is important to incorporate a virtual component because this will be a part of the learning, especially for those who are not used to using technology.

Keep in mind that we must Leverage Technology because we no longer live in an analog culture.

Churches that are able to do this may be able to increase their Leverage Technology level to 5 for Chasm Crossers.

Summary of Results for Chasm Crossers

Chasm Factor	Current Crossers	New Crossers
Focused Vision	1	5
Highlight Discovery	2	4
Product Excellence	1	3
Engaging Experience	1	5
Personal Perspective	3	4
Leverage Technology	1	5
Totals	9/30	26/30
Percent	30%	87%

The point of creating these charts that indicate current practice vs potential practice regarding the chasm factors is to give examples of how it could be done. By applying numbers (even ones that are just rough estimates) to a ministry element, like training Chasm Crossers, it helps us get a better picture of the actual situation and points out areas for improvement.

Of the four examples we have looked at I believe this one has the worst record in churches. It has been my experience that few churches providing good training for members on how they can be Chasm Crossers. Room for improvement in this area is huge.

In it together!

There is no way that most individuals in churches, by themselves, can make the personal changes necessary to become Chasm Crosse. We are going to have to do this thing together. It requires committed leaders. We need to experience the truth of the gospel again. Intercession and prayer are critical. Churches must rediscover their mission. We must listen to the Holy Spirit, understand the chasm and begin to see change as a positive thing. There are no simple fixes, but together we can turn the corner.

When I sent out the first few draft copies of this book for review, it was the parts where I talked about technology that created the most problems in the minds of the readers. They understood very well their digital deficit and this made the different scenarios I talked about seem impossible. As a technology instructor for many years, I can assure you and them, that this barrier can be overcome. I know we can do this thing, despite the challenges it brings. Remember, with God, all things are possible.

Chasm Crossers

The chasm is crossable. We can do this thing! Now is the time to take our eyes off the barriers and look for the path God has called us to take. Together we can make the changes necessary to bring about a revitalization of churches. We can create congregations that connect to the current society and make an impact in our world.

Conclusion

The process of implementing the changes that will make our churches relevant to today's Western society will be difficult, but it is necessary for churches that want to reach their communities effectively. I pray this book has provided you with a better picture of what the major issues are and just what has happened to put us in the position we are now in. Using this information, all of us together can change and make a better tomorrow. After all, this is what Christianity has always been about.

There are many other critical things that need to happen in the church in order for us to see renewal. What I hope this book has done is highlight an area that, in addition to everything else, is also critical. We must become Chasm-Crossing people who understand the culture to which we will witness. The gospel never changes, but our methods to reach others must. We must become Chasm Crossers.

References

Chapter 1 - Hearts Transformed

Bibby, Reginald. 2012. *A New Day: The Resilience & Restructuring of Religion in Canada*. Lethbridge: A Project Canada Book

George, Bob. 1989. *Classic Christianity*. Harvest House Publishers.

Lovelace, Richard. 2007. *Dynamics of Spiritual Life: An Evangelical Theology of Renewal*. Downers Grove: Intervarsity Press.

McNeal, Reggie. 2000. *A Work of Heart: Understanding How God Shapes Spiritual Leaders*. San Francisco. Jossey-Bass Publishers.

New International Version. 2011. BibleGateway.com. March 2015

Penner, James, Rachael harder, Erika Anderson, Bruno Désorcy, and Rick Hiemstra. 2011. *Hemorrhaging Faith: Why and When Canadian Adults are Leaving, Staying and Returning to Church*. Commissioned by The EFC Youth and Young Adult Ministry Roundtable.

Pew Research Center. 2013. Canada's Changing Religious Landscape. Accessed April 21, 2015 http://www.pewforum.org/2013/06/27/canadas-changing-religious-landscape/

Chapter 2 - Falling Numbers

Gardner, Harry, Editor. 2002. Year Book of the Conventions of Atlantic Baptist Churches. http://baptist-atlantic.ca/tools-resources/yearbooks/ Saint John, NB.

Green, Hollis. 1972. *Why Churches Die: A Guide to Basic Evangelism and Church Growth*. Bethany Fellowship.

Rainer, Thom. 2014. *Autopsy of a Deceased Church: 12 Ways to Keep Yours Alive*. Broadman and Holman.

Roozen, David A. 2013. "*Negative numbers: the decline narrative reaches evangelicals.*" Christian Century 130, no. 25: 10-11. ATLA Religion Database with ATLASerials, EBSCOhost (accessed April 21, 2015).

Reid, Peter, Editor. 2014. Year Book of the Conventions of Atlantic Baptist Churches. http://baptist-atlantic.ca/tools-resources/yearbooks/ Saint John, NB.

Chapter 3 - Church Health

Boulder Colorado. *Mass Casualty Triage Scale.* http://bcn.boulder.co.us/community/explorer/ep493d4c.htm

Kinnaman, David. 2011. *You Lost Me: Why Young Christians Are Leaving Church*. Baker Books

References

McNeal, Reggie. 2003. *The Present Future: Six Tough Questions for the Church.* San Francisco: Jossey-Bass.

Chapter 4 - New Market

Blank, Steve and Dorf, Bob. 2012. *The Startup Owner's Manual: the Step-by-Step Guide for Building a Great Company.* K & S Ranch, Inc.

Malphurs, Aubrey. 2013. *Look Before You Lead: How to Discern and Shape Your Church Culture.* Baker Books.

Maurya, Ash. 2012. *Running Lean: Iterate from plan A to a plan that works.* O'Reilly Media

Moore, Geoffrey. 2013. *Crossing the Chasm: Marketing and Selling Disruptive Products to Mainstream Customers.* Harpercollins Publishers

Chapter 5 - Preparing Minds

Boyatzis, Richard. Smith, Melvin. Van Oosten, Ellen. June 2010. *Coaching for Change: A case study on how Coaching with Compassion can transform organizations as opposed to the traditional approach of Coaching for Compliance.* People Matters magazine.

Boyatzis, Richard E., Smith, Melvin L., & Beveridge, Alim J. 2013. *Coaching with compassion: Inspiring health, well-being, and development in organizations.* The Journal of Applied Behavioral Science, 49, 153-178. doi:10.1177/0021886312462236

Boyatzis, Richard E. 2006. *Intentional Change Theory from a Complexity Perspective*. Journal of Management Development, 25 (7) 607-623

Boyatzis, Richard. 2013. *Inspiring Leadership through Emotional Intelligence*
coursera online course. www.coursera.com

Camp, Jim. 2012. *Decisions Are Emotional, not Logical: The Neuroscience behind Decision Making*. www.thinkbig.com

Goleman, Daniel. 2000. *Working with Emotional Intelligence*. Bantam.

Van Oosten, Ellen. and Boyatzis, Richard. 2003. *Building the Emotionally Intelligent Organization*. Ivey Business Journal.

Smith, Daniel P. and Sellon, Mary K. 2008. *Pathway to Renewal: Practical Steps for Congregations*. Herndon, VA: Alban Institute.

Snyder, Howard A. 2005. *Radical Renewal: The Problem of Wineskins Today*. Eugene, OR: Wipf & Stock.

Chapter 6 - Modern Science

Bestebreurtje, F P. 2013. "Limits of reason and limits of faith: hermeneutical considerations on evolution theology." Neue Zeitschrift Für Systematische Theologie Und Religionsphilosophie 55, no. 2: 243-257. ATLA Religion

References

Database with ATLASerials, EBSCOhost (accessed December 19, 2014).

Bozeman, Theodore Dwight. 1977. *Protestants in an Age of Science*. The University of North Carolina Press.

Brooke, Hedley John. 1991. *Science and Religion: Some Historical Perspectives*. Cambridge University Press.

CBC radio, Ideas. 2010. Looking Up. http://www.cbc.ca/ideas/episodes/features/2010/03/19/looking-up-part-1-cd/

Collins, Francis. 2006. *The Language of God: A Scientist Presents Evidence for Belief*. Free Press.

Coyne, Jerry. 2009. *Why Evolution is True*. Penguin Books.

Committee on Revising Science and Creationism. 2013. *Science, Evolution, and Creationism*. A View from the National Academy of Sciences and Institute of Medicine of the National Academies

Dawkins, Richard. 1986. *The Blind Watchmaker*. Penguin Books.

Draper, John William. 1881. *History of the Conflict Between Religion and Science*. A Public Domain Book.

Enns, Peter. 2012. *The Evolution of Adam: What The Bible Does and Doesn't Say About Human Origins*. Brazos Press.

Noll, Mark. 2000. *Turning Points: Decisive Moments in the History of Christianity*. Baker Academic.

Ostrowick, John M. 2013. "Does evolution really threaten religion?." Journal Of Theology For Southern Africa no. 146: 79-103. ATLA Religion Database with ATLASerials, EBSCOhost (accessed December 19, 2014).

Peters, Ted and Hewlett, Martinez. 2008. *Can You Believe in God and Evolution?: A Guide for the Perplexed*. Abingdon Press

Polkinghorne, John. 2005. *Exploring Reality: The Intertwining of Science and Religion*. Yale University Press.

Ruse, Michael. 2001. *Can a Darwinian be a Christian? The Relationship Between Science and Religion*. Cambridge University Press.

Ruse, Michael. 2005. *The Evolution-Creation Struggle*. Harvard University Press.

Stark, Rodney. 2004. *For the Glory of God: How Monotheism Led to Reformations, Science, Witch-Hunts, and the End of Slavery*. Princeton University Press.

Stark, Rodney. 2007. *The Victory of Reason: How Christianity Led to Freedom, Capitalism, and Western Success*. Random House.

2012. "The evolution of the debate: we haven't always been deeply divided about origins." Christianity Today 56, no. 7: 28-29. ATLA Religion Database with ATLASerials, EBSCOhost (accessed December 19, 2014).

Wilcox, David. 2004. *God and Evolution: A Faith-Based Understanding*. Judson Press.

References

Chapter 7 - Productive Society

Bell Jr., Daniel. 2012. *The Economy of Desire: Christianity and Capitalism in a Postmodern World*. Baker Academic.

Baumol, William and Alan Blinder. 2016. *Economics Principles and Policy*. Cengage Learning.

Butler, Eamonn. 2011. *The Condensed Wealth of Nations and the Incredibly Condensed Theory of Moral Sentiments*. Adam Smith Institute.

Connolly, William. 2008. *Capitalism and Christianity, American Style*. Duke University Press.

Diamond, Jared. 1999. *Guns, Germs, and Steel: The Fates of Human Societies*. W. W. Norton & company.

Gregory, Brad. 2012. *The Unintended Reformation: How a Religious Revolution Secularized Society*. Harvard University Press.

Jethani, Skye. 2010. "The unholy trinity of consumerism." Cultural Encounters 6, no. 1: 79-85. ATLA Religion Database with ATLASerials, EBSCOhost (accessed December 19, 2014).

Novak, Michael. How Christianity Created Capitalism. Action Institute for the Study of Religion and Liberty. http://www.acton.org/pub/religion-liberty/volume-10-number-3/how-christianity-created-capitalism (Accessed Dec 2014).

Nye, John 2008. "Standards of Living and Modern Economic Growth." *The Concise Encyclopedia of Economics*. Liberty Fund, Inc http://www.econlib.org/library/Enc/StandardsofLivingandModernEconomicGrowth.html (Accessed April 2015).

Palaian, Sally. 2009. S*pent: Breaking the Buying Obsession and Discovering Your True Worth*. Hazelden

Shmoop Editorial Team. 2008. The Gilded Age Learning Guide Shmoop.com http://www.shmoop.com/gilded-age/summary.html (retrieved, December 2014).

Stark, Rodney. 2014. How the West Won: The Neglected Story of the Triumph of Modernity. Intercollegiate Studies Institute.

Stark, Rodney. 2007. *(The Victory of Reason: How Christianity Led to Freedom, Capitalism, and Western Success*. Random House.

Stark, Rodney. 2005. Article: How Christianity Led to Freedom, Capitalism, and the Success of the West. Catholic Education Resource Center
http://www.catholiceducation.org/en/culture/catholic-contributions/how-christianity-led-to-freedom-capitalism-and-the-success-of-the-west.html

Weber, Max, author. Parsons, Talcott, translator. 1992. *The Protestant Ethic and the Spirit of Capitalism*. Routledge

Wikipedia. December 2014. "Gilded Age." http://en.wikipedia.org/wiki/Gilded_Age

Chapter 8 - Human Freedom

References

Alcorn, Randy. 1985. *Christians in the Wake of the Sexual Revolution: Recovering Our Sexual Sanity*. Multnomah Press.

Barzel, Yoram. 1977. "An Economic Analysis of Slavery." *Journal of Law and Economics.*, Vol. 20, No. 1 (Apr., 1977), pp. 87-110

Cross, Gary. 1990. *A Social History of Leisure since 1600*. Venture Publishing, Inc.

Firth, Simon. 1981. *Sound Effects: Youth, Leisure, and the Politics of Rock 'n' Roll*. New York: Pantheon Books

Gardella, Peter. 1985. *Innocent Ecstasy: How Christianity Gave America an Ethic of Sexual Pleasure*. Oxford University Press.

Giordano, Ralph. 2003. *Fun and Games in Twentieth-Century America*. Greenwood Press.

Harris, George. 1886. "The American development of leisure." Andover Review (Boston, Mass.) 6, no. 32: 184-188. ATLA Religion Database with ATLASerials, EBSCOhost (accessed December 19, 2014).

Hoch, Stephen. 1989. *Serfdom and Social Control in Russia: Petrovskoe, a Village in Tambov*. University of Chicago Press

Kallestad, Walt. 1996. *Entertainment Evangelism: Taking the Church Public*. Nashville: Abingdon Press.

Katz, Mark. 2004. *Capturing Sound: How Technology has Changed Music*. University of California Press.

Kilde, Jeanne Halgren. 2003. "American Protestantism and leisure." Religious Studies Review 29, no. 2: 151-157. ATLA Religion

Database with ATLASerials, EBSCOhost (accessed December 19, 2014).

Kuehne, Dale S. 2009. *Sex and the iWorld: Rethinking Relationship beyond an Age of Individualism*. Grand Rapids: Baker Academic.

Leibovitz, Liel. 2014. God in the Machine: Video Games as Spiritual Pursuit. templeton Press.

Moogk, Edward and Théberge, Paul. *Recorded Sound Technology and its Impact*. Historica Canada.
http://www.thecanadianencyclopedia.ca/en/article/recorded-sound-technology-and-its-impact-emc/

Postman, Neil. 1985. *Amusing Ourselves to Death*. Toronto: Penguin.

Reichert, Tom. 2003. *The Erotic History of Advertising*. Prometheus Books.

Schut, Kevin. 2013. *Of Games and God: A Christian Exploration of Video Games*. Brazos Press.

Stark, Rodney. 2013. *The Truth About the Catholic Church and Slavery*.
http://www.christianitytoday.com/ct/2003/julyweb-only/7-14-53.0.html

Chapter 9 - Individual Truth

Bechtle, Mike. 2006. *Evangelism for the Rest of Us*. Grand Rapids: Baker.

References

Dorsett, Terry W. 2012. *Mission Possible: Reaching the Next Generation Through the Small Church.* Bloomington, IN: CrossBooks.

Elofson, Matt. 2004-2005. "Navigating Our Shifting Culture: A New Horizon for Evangelism in a Postmodern Context." *Journal of the Academy for Evangelism in Theological Education.* Vol. 20: 32-41. ATLA Religion Database with ATLASerials, EBSCOhost (accessed September 1, 2014).

Fitch, David. 2001-2002. "Saving Souls Beyond Modernity: How Evangelism Can Save the Church and Make it Relevant Again." *Journal of the Academy for Evangelism in Theological Education.* Vol. 17: 17-33. ATLA Religion Database with ATLASerials, EBSCOhost (accessed September 1, 2014).

Fosdick, Harry Emerson. 1922. *"Shall the Fundamentalists Win?"* http://historymatters.gmu.edu/d/5070/

Grassie, William. 1997. "Postmodernism : What One Needs to Know." Zygon 32, no. 1: 83-94. ATLA Religion Database with ATLASerials, EBSCOhost (accessed November 3, 2014).

Günther, Wolfgang. 1997. "Postmodernism." International Review Of Mission 86, no. 343: 425-431. ATLA Religion Database with ATLASerials, EBSCOhost (accessed November 3, 2014).

Hastings, Ross. 2012. *Missional God, Missional Church: Hope for Re-Evangelizing the West.* Downers Grove: IVP Academic.

Hoekema, David A. and Gong, Bobby. 1997. *Christianity and Culture in the Crossfire.* Grand Rapids: Calvin College.

Hoffman, Louis. 2008. Premodernism, Modernism, & Postmodernism: An Overview. (accessed Nov 5, 2014) http://www.postmodernpsychology.com/philosophical_systems/overview.htm

Hunter, George G., III. 2003-2004. "Six ways churches Grow." *Journal of the Academy for Evangelism in Theological Education.* Vol. 19: 63-77. ATLA Religion Database with ATLASerials, EBSCOhost (accessed September 1, 2014).

Hunter, George G., III. 2000. *The Celtic Way of Evangelism: How Christianity Can Reach the West...Again.* Abingdon Press.

Keller, Tim (2012). Center Church: Doing Balanced Gospel-Based Ministry in Your City. Grand Rapids: Zondervan.

Kerr, Hugh Thomson. 1990. "[Modernism and postmodernism]." Theology Today 47, no. 2: 131-164. ATLA Religion Database with ATLASerials, EBSCOhost (accessed November 3, 2014).

The Manila Manifesto. 1989. Available online: http://www.lausanne.org/en/documents/manila-manifesto.html

McNeal, Reggie. 2003. *The Present Future: Six Tough Questions for the Church.* John Wiley & Sons.

Moreau, A. Scott. 2012. *Contextualization in World Missions: Mapping and Assessing Evangelical Models.* Grand Rapids: Kregel Publications.

Nelson, Gary V. 2009. *Borderland Churches: A Congregation's Introduction to Missional Living.* St. Louis: Chalice Press.

Newbigin, Lesslie. 1986. *Foolishness to the Greeks.* Grand Rapids: Eerdmans.

References

Newbigin, Lesslie. 1989. *The Gospel in a Pluralist Society*. Grand Rapids: Eerdmans.

Newman, Randy. 2004. *Questioning Evangelism*. Kregel Publications.

Niebuhr, Richard. 1951. Christ and Culture. New York: Harper & Row, Publishers.

Richardson, Rick. 2010. "Evangelism and Social Concern: How Do We Maintain a Healthy Balance?" *Journal of the Academy for Evangelism in Theological Education*. Vol. 24: 19-34. ATLA Religion Database with ATLASerials, EBSCOhost (accessed September 1, 2014).

Poe, Harry L. 2001. *Christian Witness in a Postmodern World*. Abingdon.

Poe, Harry L. 2004. *See No Evil: The Existence of Sin in an Age of Relativism*. Grand Rapids: Kregel Publications.

Reid, Alvin L., 2002. *Radically Unchurched: Who They Are & How to Reach Them*. Kregel Publications.

Redeeming the Arts. The Restoration of the Arts to God's Creational Intention. Lausanne Occasional Paper No. 46. Available online: http://www.lausanne.org/docs/2004forum/LOP46_IG17.pdf

Sousa, Rodrigo de. 2003. "Rethinking an evangelical response to postmodernism: a critique and proposal." Presbyterian 29, no. 2: 94-102. ATLA Religion Database with ATLASerials, EBSCOhost (accessed November 3, 2014).

Stetzer, Ed. 2003. *Planting New Churches in a Postmodern Age*. Broadman & Holman Publishers.

Stiver, Dan R. 2002. "Much ado about Athens and Jerusalem: the implications of postmodernism for faith." Review & Expositor 99, no. 3: 395-416. ATLA Religion Database with ATLASerials, EBSCOhost (accessed November 3, 2014).

Van Gelder, Craig and Zscheile, Dwight 2011. *The Missional Church in Perspective*. Grand Rapids: Baker Academic.

Wikipedia, Empiriscism
http://en.wikipedia.org/wiki/Empiricism

Wikipedia, Modern History
http://en.wikipedia.org/wiki/Modern_history#Pre-Modern

Wikpedia, Scientific method
http://en.wikipedia.org/wiki/Scientific_method

Wikpedia, Special Relativity
http://en.wikipedia.org/wiki/Special_relativity

Chapter 10 - Digitally Connected

Bainbridge, William Sims and Bainbridge, Wilma Alice. 2007. "Electronic Game Research Methodologies: Studying Religious Implications," *Review of Religious Research*, 49:1, 35-53.

Challies, Tim. 2011. *The Next Story: Life and Faith After the Digital Explosion*. Grand Rapids: Zondervan.

Cheong, Pauline Hope; Fischer-Nielson, Peter; Gelfgren, Stefan; and Ess, Charles; editors 2012. *Digital Religion, Social Media, and Culture*. New York: Peter Lang Publishing.

References

Cheong, Pauline Hope; Poon, Jessie P. H.; Huang, Shirlena; Casas, Irene. 2009. "The Internet Highway and Religious Communities: Mapping and Contesting Spaces in Religion-Online," *The Information Society*, 25:5, 291 – 302.

Detweiler, Craig. 2013. *iGods. How Technology Shapes our Spiritual and Social Lives*. Grand Rapids: Brazos.

Drescher, Elizabeth. 2011. *Tweet If You ♥ Jesus: Practicing Church in the Digital Age*. New York: Morehouse Publishing.

Educause Learning Initiative. 2005. "7 things you should know about blogs,"
https://net.educause.edu/ir/library/pdf/ELI7006.pdf

Educause Learning Initiative. 2005. "7 things you should know about collaborative editing,"
https://net.educause.edu/ir/library/pdf/ELI7009.pdf

Educause Learning Initiative. 2006. "7 things you should know about Facebook,"
https://net.educause.edu/ir/library/pdf/ELI7017.pdf

Educause Learning Initiative. 2007. "7 things you should know about Facebook II,"
https://net.educause.edu/ir/library/pdf/ELI7025.pdf

Educause Learning Initiative. 2005. "7 things you should know about instant messaging,"
https://net.educause.edu/ir/library/pdf/ELI7008.pdf

Educause Learning Initiative. 2005. "7 things you should know about podcasting,"
https://net.educause.edu/ir/library/pdf/ELI7003.pdf

Educause Learning Initiative. 2010. "7 things you should know about privacy in web 2.0 learning environments," https://net.educause.edu/ir/library/pdf/ELI7064.pdf

Educause Learning Initiative. 2005. "7 things you should know about wikis," https://net.educause.edu/ir/library/pdf/ELI7004.pdf

Educause Learning Initiative. 2006. "7 things you should know about Youtube," https://net.educause.edu/ir/library/pdf/ELI7018.pdf

Mashable. October 2014. "A Brief History of Instant Messaging," http://mashable.com/2012/10/25/instant-messaging-history/

McLuhan, Eric and Szklarek, Jacek. 1999. *The Medium and the Light. Reflections on Religion. Marshall McLuhan.* Eugene, OR: Wipf and Stock.

McLuhan, Marshall. 1964 rpt. 1994. *Understanding Media: The Extensions of Man.* Cambridge, MA: MIT Press.

Postman, Neil. 1993. *Technopoly: The Surrender of Culture to Technology.* New York: Vintage Books.

Purcell, Kristen. 2011. Search and email still top the list of most popular online activities. http://www.pewinternet.org/2011/08/09/search-and-email-still-top-the-list-of-most-popular-online-activities/

Rainie, Lee and Wellman, Barry. 2012. *Networked: The New Social Media Operating System.* Cambridge, MA: MIT Press.

Turkle, Sherry. 2011. *Alone Together.* New York: Basic Books.

References

VonBuseck, Craig. 2010. *Netcasters: Using the Internet to Make Fishers of Men.* Nashville: Broadman and Holman.

Wikipedia. October 2014. "Amazon.com."
http://en.wikipedia.org/wiki/Amazon.com

Wikipedia. October 2014. "Email."
http://en.wikipedia.org/wiki/Email

Wikipedia. October 2014. "Facebook."
http://en.wikipedia.org/wiki/Facebook

Wikipedia. October 2014. "History of the Internet."
http://en.wikipedia.org/wiki/History_of_the_Internet

Wikipedia. October 2014. "History of Wikis."
http://en.wikipedia.org/wiki/History_of_wikis

Wikipedia. October 2014. "Instant Messaging."
http://en.wikipedia.org/wiki/Instant_messaging

Wikipedia. October 2014. "MOOC."
http://en.wikipedia.org/wiki/Massive_open_online_course

Wikipedia. October 2014. "Youtube."
http://en.wikipedia.org/wiki/YouTube

http://en.wikipedia.org/wiki/YouTube

Wikipedia. October 2014. "Zynga."
    http://en.wikipedia.org/wiki/Zynga

www.ingramcontent.com/pod-product-compliance
Lightning Source LLC
Chambersburg PA
CBHW050631160426
43194CB00010B/1631